ART NOUVEAU and ART DECO

BY GEOFFREY WARREN AND DAN KLEIN

Galley Press

This edition published 1978 by
Galley Press
In association with Cathay Books
59 Grosvenor Street, London W1

© 1974, 1978 Hennerwood Publications Limited

ISBN 0 904644 64 2

Produced by Mandarin Publishers Limited
22a Westlands Road
Quary Bay, Hong Kong

Printed in Hong Kong

CONTENTS

ALL COLOR BOOK OF ART NOUVEAU

BY GEOFFREY WARREN

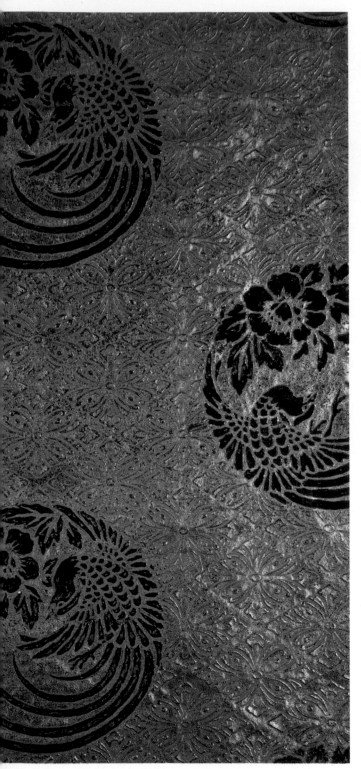

INTRODUCTION

Think of a sensuous line; of a flowing line; a line which bends and turns back on itself. Think of the feminine form, rounded and curving. Think of plant forms growing and burgeoning. Think of flowers in bud, in overblown blossom, as seed pods. Think of lines which seem not to conform; think of waves, think of women's hair; think of twisting smoke. Think too, of controlled lines: lines which begin parallel but then converge and eventually contradict each other. Think of the resulting stress. As the English artist, Walter Crane, one of the earliest exponents of the 'New Art' said in 1889: 'Line is all-important. Let the designer, therefore, in the adaptation of his art, lean upon the staff of line—line determinative, line emphatic, line delicate, line expressive, line controlling and uniting.'

Then think of all this expressed in architecture, rooms, furniture, ceramics, glass, jewellery, the printed page, posters, coffee pots, lamps and cutlery and you will have some idea what Art Nouveau is all about.

But think first of what at the end of the nineteenth century it was *not*. All over that part of the civilized world which had emerged from the Industrial Revolution every upper or middle class home was stuffed with furniture and objects which were copied from Classical, Renaissance, Baroque and Rococco styles. For the most part they were vulgar copies, products of an increasing industrialization, produced for a *nouveau riche* class, which wanted to be reassured that it could afford 'safe', already accepted 'works of art.' Their houses were as affected outside as inside by this desire, as were their town halls, museums, railway stations, and libraries which resembled Greek temples, Renaissance palaces or Gothic churches.

But a reaction was inevitable. Many artists became sick of imitative art and of the machine which seemed to have debased and coarsened everything. They wanted to return to craftsmanship, simplicity and 'nature'. They wanted the products of contemporary civilization to be truly representative of it. As Otto Wagner, a German Architect wrote in 1895, the 'New Style' was to be not a *rebirth*, but a *birth*: modern life alone must be the starting point of artistic creation. This premise was never completely carried out; one must admit that many Art Nouveau artists *did* go back, but in the main they created objects which were valid in themselves and genuinely expressed the age in which they were conceived. The period of this 'New Style' was very short: at its purest, a mere twenty years, from about 1890 to 1910. But for all its brevity, it was one of the most original manifestations of the human creative spirit. Even if one cannot always applaud it, one must admire its audacity and courage.

But no period of art arrives complete and ready-made. There are always influences working, often centuries back. One can trace Art Nouveau ideas in Celtic, Gothic, Rococco and Japanese art. The Industrial Revolution upset the balance of a natural progression from one art period to another by making reproduction of past forms all too easy. Rumblings of discontent can be traced to writers in the late eighteenth century when the machine began to take over, but it was left to the 1851 Exhibition at the Crystal Palace in London to set off the first blast of real reaction.

Here we discover a paradox. The Crystal Palace, that greenhouse brain-child of the Prince Consort and Joseph Paxton was in itself a revolutionary step. Iron and glass were used to create a simple, startling, functional statement. It looked like a fairy bubble; but it was a bubble which worked. Ironically the contents which it housed, gathered from all over the world, did not measure up to their packing. All the products so proudly displayed were then considered to be in the best 'good taste.' It was left to William Morris, an inspired, far-seeing and socialistic artist, to call it 'tons upon tons of unutterable rubbish.'

Morris is the touchstone for the Art Nouveau movement; yet even he was influenced by the writer John Ruskin and the Pre-Raphaelite painters. Ruskin, hating the machine and the modern world, wanted to retreat to the Middle Ages. In this he was misguided, as were the Pre-Raphaelites, who fondly imagined that they were reproducing the 'pure' Medieval world before Raphael. They believed that only 'nature' was acceptable and on this they turned a microscopic eye. They also hoped, through their art, to reform a materialistic world.

But William Morris went further. Turning his back on the hated machine he preached Art for All, not art as a rare thing which would be produced by only an 'artist'. *Every* man, in his view, was an artist. He had only to return to the Middle Ages, when craftsmanship reigned supreme, to be able to produce objects which were indisputably beautiful.

In 1861, Morris, in collaboration with others, set up the Arts and Crafts Movement. Everything was to be handmade. Furniture, tapestries, wallpapers, fabrics, pottery: all had to be objects of beauty *and* use. The joy of the craftsman in his work would ensure that the work itself was beautiful. And this beauty would immediately be accepted and appreciated by the buyer. Morris wanted art for everyone, just as he wanted education and freedom for everyone.

But he did not realize that hand-made products would be far too expensive for the masses, who, under increasing industrialization were becoming even poorer. He did not appreciate that Victorian society was in no way comparable to the Medieval one. Sincere as he was, his vision was doomed to failure.

But he did set the ball rolling. Without his vision, few of the succeeding Arts and Crafts Societies, the shops, the Arts Centres, the schools, the exhibitions, the magazines and journals, would have happened. One of his most imaginative disciples was Arthur H. Mackmurdo, who founded the Century Guild in 1881. Like Morris, he was typical of the 'new' artist, in that he designed *all* forms of domestic articles. This diversification was to be the outstanding hall-

Introduction

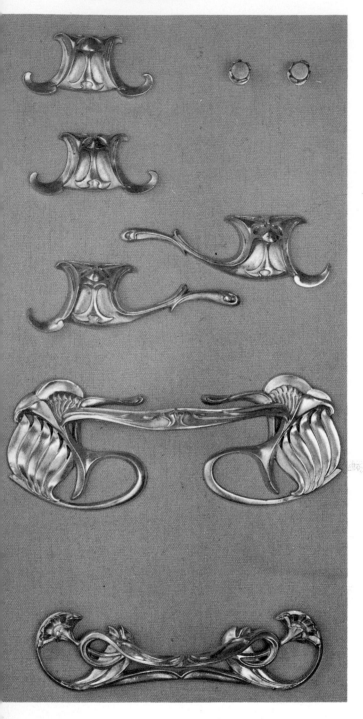

mark of succeeding Art Nouveau artists. There were few who were not able to design a knife and fork with the same fervour, skill and enthusiasm that they put into a building, a piece of furniture or a painting.

Other groups soon followed. Walter Crane, book-designer and illustrator, founded the Art Workers' Guild in 1884. The Arts and Crafts Exhibition Society and the Guild of Handicrafts, the latter inaugurated by C. R. Ashbee, were started in 1899.

For another Art Nouveau influence we must turn to the American painter, James McNeil Whistler. If it had not been for his interest in Japanese Art, this important influence in Art Nouveau might not have been so strong. From the Orient he took its subtle colours, its spare, attenuated line and its masterly use of space. He decorated his own house in Japanese style in 1863 and again 1867. Between 1867 and 1877 he designed the famous peacock room (now in the Freer Gallery of Art, Smithsonian Institution, Washington), inspired by that bird which was to be such a recurring motif for Art Nouveau artists. He also designed a room as a *whole*.

It was this theory of one designer creating a room or an entire house in one style that was one of Art Nouveau's contributions to interior decoration. At once a success and a failure, at its best it succeeded; at its worst a whole room, particularly in the most extreme Art Nouveau style, is often too overwhelming and too restless to be lived with. So writhing and contorted were some rooms, so overloaded with decoration and design, so constructed out of apparently growing plant forms, that one must have felt in danger of being swallowed up by some enchanted fairy forest.

Because, as with so many revolutions, previous faults were repeated in a different manner, many people soon turned away from Art Nouveau. As a result, few rooms still exist in their entirety.

In 1862 an exhibition of Japanese goods was held in Paris. The whole stand was subsequently bought by an English firm, who put Arthur Lazenby Liberty in charge of their new Oriental department in London. When the firm closed, in 1874, Mr Liberty bought its stock and opened his own shop in Regent Street. Thus the famous firm was born, and thus, due to the fact that Liberty and Co. patronized and encouraged Art Nouveau artists, the name *Stile Liberty* was given to the movement at one of its stages.

The initial impetus therefore, was English, and its earliest exponent in England was the already mentioned Arthur Mackmurdo. His first Art Nouveau venture was for a chairback, all sweeping curves, which he designed as early as 1881 (see plate 4). He followed it by numerous fabrics, wallpapers and items of furniture. In 1883 he executed a title-page for a book on Christopher Wren's City Churches. Mackmurdo's design had nothing to do with its subject but, like the chairback, it was in Art Nouveau style with its flame-like plant forms, attenuated peacocks and lettering incorporated in the design.

In architecture and furniture Mackmurdo used a narrow vertical line which was to influence such architects as Voysey and Mackintosh. His stylization took natural forms and translated them into abstraction, without losing the original inspiration.

C. R. Ashbee, architect and silversmith (see page *51*), produced the typical English solution to life and art: that of compromise. Closely allied to the Arts and Crafts movement he was also an important influence on early Art Nouveau.

Charles Annesley Voysey was another English artist at whom the rather unflattering title of 'compromiser' can be levied. Influenced by Japanese art, he excelled in domestic architecture and his houses were particularly successful in their precise proportions, subtle asymmetry and understated ornament. He also used a heart-shaped decorative device— the shape which had a phallic symbolism: the natural concomitant to the female motifs so much used by the whole Movement.

Like prophets, many of these English artists and architects received more recognition abroad than in their own country. Such a one was Hugh Ballie Scott, furniture designer and architect who used Art Nouveau elements as design on flat surfaces rather than on whole pieces (see plate *31*).

Aubrey Beardsley, one of the most famous of English artists has, through recent popularization, become synonymous with Art Nouveau. But we must distinguish between those artists who worked solely from Art Nouveau principles and those who, though using Art Nouveau shapes and motifs, were not actually *of* the Movement. As with Toulouse-Lautrec, Beardsley was a genius in his own right and used Art Nouveau to suit his purpose. His illustrations for Oscar Wilde's *Salome* with their Japanese feeling, stylized women, roses and peacocks are a case in point.

Although it was principally English reaction to the accepted mode, the influence of the Arts and Crafts Movement and like guilds, which persuaded Continental artists also to rebel, little of any importance was later produced in England, although it was kept alive and encouraged by *The Studio* journal and by Liberty in his shop in Regent Street.

Because of his rule that little of the work sold in his shop should be signed it is difficult to attribute English products with certainty. Pewter marked Tubric and silver marked Cymbric came from him; for the rest one has to look for objects which display a certain restraint. On the credit side Liberty made Art Nouveau popular; on the debit, he encouraged poor imitations and unsuitable mass-production.

The journal *The Studio*, with its reports of exhibitions all over Europe gave huge support to Art Nouveau. It also set competitions for a wall-sconce, a fountain or a fire-place. And the amateurs who entered, produced results which are strongly Art Nouveau. This aspect, regrettably, gave the movement a bad name and also hastened its end as a fashionable art form. Professionals cannot bear amateurs!

English designers and artists exhibited their new-found freedom at Brussels in the late 1880's and also in 1892: it was in this year that one of the brightest stars of the Movement, the Belgian architect Victor Norta (1861–1947), began to plan the first important Continental house to be built in Art Nouveau style. This was the Maison Tassel in Brussels. Completed in 1893 it is a watershed of Art Nouveau design, combining as it does both two- and three-dimensional architectural features and decoration. He used wrought-iron in a new way: particularly in the staircase for this house, a poem of fairy-like tendrils, plant forms being his chief source of inspiration. He paid Mackmurdo the com-

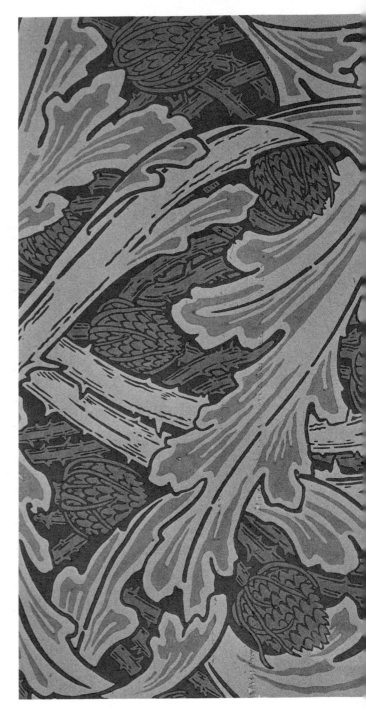

Plate 2

Voysey, one of the first English designers to take William Morris's interpretation of Medieval designs one step nearer to Art Nouveau principles, is credited with designing this simple swirling design of teasles, translated in subtle pinks and browns. His designs were less Medieval-inspired than those of Morris, and have a more linear, flat quality.

Introduction

Plate 3

A very important early precursor of the whole Art Nouveau movement, this chair-back by Arthur Heygate Mackmurdo (1851–1942) the English designer, was made as early as 1881. All his designs displayed a completely new concept: a strong sense of rhythm which, taking one direction, would suddenly and dramatically change course, setting up a tension never to be lost in subsequent Art Nouveau design. The chair is an ordinary Victorian one transformed by the pierced and swirly back. Behind it in the photograph are a screen and a carpet by him.

pliment of using one of his wallpapers in this house. Horta designed other important buildings in Brussels: the Hotel van Etvelde in 1898, the Hotel Solvay and the Maison du Peuple in 1895–1900. The latter is remarkable for its façade of iron and glass.

Another Belgian, Henri van de Velde (1863–1957), was not lacking in courage himself in rejecting nineteenth-century cultural pastiche. Starting as a painter he soon displayed an interest in furniture, house decoration, tapestry, silver and jewellery. He strictly followed the tenet that the nature of the material must determine the form and the decoration of whatever subject was involved.

It was from France, pioneer of so many world-affecting art forms, that there came some of the most sophisticated and eccentric manifestations of Art Nouveau. The name of the Movement was finally settled in the French tongue and many of its foremost artists and architects took up the new style. They, of all artists, caught Walter Crane's definition of Art Nouveau as a 'disease' in its most virulent form. Paris, cultural apex of the world, became one of the centres for this newest of crazes and either excelled in it or descended to producing artifacts at their most impractical and bizarre.

The Paris Exhibition of 1900 marked the height of the capital's power and influence; from this moment it reigned supreme in the *Modern Style*, outdoing nearly all others in the way it had always done. Did not the 'Divine' Sarah Bernhardt patronize Mucha and Lalique? Had not Oscar Wilde, most cosmopolitan of writers, written his *Salome* in French? Had not Beardsley, the most French-influenced of English artists, matched the book with perverse and scandalous illustrations? Had not Toulouse-Lautrec elevated the music hall, the stage, prostitutes and lesbians onto the sacred heights of pure art, in his paintings, posters and lithographs?

But not even the French could deny their debt to England and Morris. Not that Paris had the monopoly of French talent: Nancy was also an important centre, producing, among others, such designers as Majorelle, the Daum Brothers and Emile Gallé. It was the latter, who, as early as 1872, visited England and drank from the inspirational fountain of the Arts and Crafts Movement. Equipped with this, his native sensitivity, and expertize inherited from a father who owned a pottery workshop, he set about perfecting a technique of glass making which was strongly to influence the course of Art Nouveau. In this, the design was covered with wax and the remaining areas eaten with acid, which achieved a double surface, both matt and shiny. This glass, with its myriad variations of colour and shading, resulting from cutting, was the very apotheosis of mystery. Greens and yellows, rose and brown, violet and orange: all the variations of smoke from thick to thin, transfigured and illuminated his vases, glasses and jugs.

Not only glass came under his spell: he also designed furniture (see plate 44). Many of his pieces were bone-shaped and he excelled in marquetry and the use of mother-of-pearl.

Another native of Nancy, Louis Majorelle followed Gallé. He worked in the tradition of French furniture design, enriching it with his particular contribution of convoluted and twisted Art Nouveau shapes often carried out in gilt and bronze. He made wood and metal suit his whims but he was always the master, never the servant, of his materials.

One of the most famous and most easily recognizable products of Art Nouveau are the Métro entrances in Paris which date from 1900. These were designed by Hector Guimard, one of the most interesting of French architects and designers. He was influenced by Horta but gave his work a special flavour inspired, as was Horta, by plant forms. His first principal architectural venture was the Castel Béranger built in Paris between 1894 and '98. The building boasts a staircase as bold and inventive as Horta's but it is in the iron gateway (see plate 25) that Guimard's genius is shown to full advantage.

In 1895, Samuel Bing, a collector of Japanese art, opened a shop in Paris which he called *La Maison de l'Art Nouveau*. Henri van de Velde is credited with coining the phrase in 1894 but it was Bing's new shop, to which so many artists flocked, that gave the Movement its official title. Bing commissioned an unknown young English artist, Frank Brangwyn, to paint murals for the shop (see plate 85). Following Bing's example many other such shops soon opened in Paris.

Not French but Czech, Alfons Mucha nevertheless found fame in Paris, largely through his posters of Sarah Bernhardt (see plate 95B). He also did work for murals, books, advertisements and magazines, as well as inspiring busts and jewellery.

It is in the realm of jewellery that Art Nouveau holds unquestioned excellence, and it is French designers such as Vever, Fouquet and above all, René Lalique, who produced the best work. Gold, obsidian, pearls, opals, enamel, diamonds, rubies, *plique à jour* and even carved glass were grist to his exotic mill. Myriads of necklaces, brooches, hair ornaments, pendants, combs and pins spun from his fertile brain. He was taken up by Bernhardt, lionized by society and given awards. He used every plant form; every aspect of the peacock; every insect and every strange creature from snake to bat; he rendered women's faces, breasts and hair. He gave solid and glittering form to such soft natural forms as the convolvulus, honesty, sycamore seeds and thistledown.

The Dutch, not very responsive to the Movement, produced some pottery by J. Jurriaan Kok (see plate 54), a building or two and some graphic design but also two important painters, Jan Toorop and Johan Thorn Prikker. They were influenced by the Pre-Raphaelites and Celtic art and idealized women in true Art Nouveau manner. Toorop's women also have a sinister, other-wordly quality in keeping with his quasi-religious themes. He was also inspired by the French Symbolist movement. Prikker, using more stylized, pattern-making techniques, had a fine sense of colour and was also obsessed by religious themes (see plate 84). Both artists show a marked English predilection for literary inspiration.

Norway also produced an artist of great stature: Edvard Munch, who studied in Paris and then spent some years in Berlin where he became the greatest influence

Plate 4

The influence of Art Nouveau soon spread to ordinary domestic architecture and interior decoration, as shown in this simple chimney piece. The fireplace, tiles and woodwork are all decorated with Art Nouveau motifs, which are repeated in the copper and ceramic ornaments, and in the wallpaper designed by Voysey. The clock, also by Voysey, is made of wood and mother-of-pearl and reflects the Mackintosh school.

on German Expressionist painting. In his use of natural forms that reflect man's oneness with, and dependance on, nature, his technique of curved, flowing lines—sometimes violent, sometimes blurred—he is close allied to the Art Nouveau Movement. His paintings reflect his feeling of jealousy, melancholy, anxiety and morbidity and in him one could say that Freud found visual expression (see plate 89).

It is strange that from Scotland, geographically and in many ways culturally, remote from Europe, that there should emerge one of the most interesting and important exponents of the Movement. Largely ignored by England he was nevertheless hailed on the Continent as one of the most important exponents of the New Style. This man was Charles Rennie Mackintosh, architect, furniture designer, painter, jeweller, et al.

Living in Glasgow he founded a famous group: 'The Four', consisting of himself, his wife Margaret, Margaret Macdonald and her sister Frances. This group was acknowledged by the Vienna Sezessionstil and exhibited there in 1897. The group also held an important exhibition at Turin in 1901. Rejecting the florid, over-rich curvilinear motifs common to most of Art Nouveau, Mackintosh and his associates went in for sound structure, simplicity, long straight lines, organized space and such cool colours as white, mauve, green and grey, often dramatically emphasized by black.

Apart from many private houses, Mackintosh designed three buildings which are now most closely connected with his name. All in Glasgow, these are the School of Art, the Willow Tea Rooms and Miss Cranston's Tea Room. Of these, only the Art School remains in its entirety. In it, Mackintosh's main influence was Scottish baronial style, to which he added delicate curving iron-work and soaring windows. In the interiors there is the clever use of contrasting planes and subtle detail. There is even a Cubist interpretation of a Doric capital in the Headmaster's room.

His Willow Tea Rooms was a masterpiece—with its white wooden doors panelled in multi-coloured glass and metal (see plate 32). For these rooms he designed everything: chairs, tables, carpets, light fittings as well as the murals.

He was most appreciated in Vienna where he exhibited interiors at the eighth Sezessionist Exhibition. Austria and Germany had been slow starters in the new Style. But the magazine Jugend gave Art Nouveau one of its other names: Jugendstil. Van de Velde lectured on the new art form at Krefeld in 1895, exhibited his own work at Dresden in 1897 and, when he moved to Berlin in 1899 to live and work, he became an acknowledged leader of the Sezessionists.

In Germany, Hermann Obrist was an artist who practised and propagated Art Nouveau. He designed a revolutionary wall hanging (see plate 5) and went on to ceramics and sculpture, creating abstract whirls and spirals out of stone and clay. Influenced by Tiffany and Gallé, the Germans also turned to glass, and Johann Lötz, with his iridescent and subtle colours most nearly resembled these two masters.

Plate 5

One of the most important and famous of all Art Nouveau products, this embroidered wall hanging, *Cyclamen*, was designed by Hermann Obrist (1863–1927) in 1895. The German magazine *Pan* described him as 'exploring the phenomena and forces of nature', and this is shown nowhere more clearly than in this example of which the same magazine wrote: 'Its frantic movement reminds us of the sudden violent curves occasioned by the crack of a whip: now appearing as a forceful outburst of the elements of nature, a stroke of lightning: now, as the defiant signature of a great man, a conqueror.' So apt was this summing up that the hanging is now generally referred to as 'The Whiplash'.

German and Austrian Art Nouveau designers had a tendency towards heaviness; they echoed British, French and Belgian models but usually lacked their delicacy. The Munich architect, August Endel, however, did create facades and interiors which writhed and curved with spindly lightness. One furniture designer to use German heaviness with success was Richard Riemerschmid whose pieces speak strong simplicity (see plate 39), foretelling much work designed later in this century.

Other Austrian architects to be influenced by Mackintosh were Peter Behrens, Josef Hoffman and Otto Wagner who was a leader of Germanic architects during the early years of this century: his Post Office Savings Bank in Vienna being built between 1904 and 1906. These architects, as well as artists, benefited from an imaginative patron, the Grand Duke of Hesse, who in 1901 invited designers to build an artist's colony at Darmstadt. Olbrich designed most of the houses for it, but many of the interiors were by Behrens. Especially notable was the library of his own house and its gentle curves and colours, the simple unity of desk, ceiling and carpet recall Mackintosh. It is easy to see how Behrens, in his turn, influenced such 'twenties and 'thirties architects as Walter Gropius and Le Corbusier.

Joseph Hoffman, who designed the Palais Stoclet in Brussels between 1905–11, which housed Klimt's masterly murals (see plate 87), also designed interiors for houses and exhibitions (whole rooms for exhibitions were a great feature of Art Nouveau) with stencilled wall decoration, tall cabinets and chairs which could almost be taken for those designed by Mackintosh.

Mention has been made of Gustav Klimt, founder member of the Vienna Sezession and one of the most interesting painters of the Movement. In his portraits and murals he usually portrayed women; but whereas most Art Nouveau women tend to be rather sexless, Klimt painted them with a disturbingly sensual reality. At the same time his work was strongly decorative, flat and almost Cubist. In fact, Austrian Art Nouveau's artists' work can be identified by a strong cubist tendency, which owes much to Mackintosh, little to France; see Moser's cabinet (plate 43). Austria's influential and highly successful magazine *Ver Sacrum*, also shows this clearly with its clean marriage of text, borders and illustrations often conceived on variations of the cube (see plate 101).

Most people have heard of Tiffany—his lamps, those stained-glass mushrooms, have become almost an Art Nouveau cliché. Son of a successful New York jeweller who had a branch of his shop in Regent Street, in London, in 1868, the young Tiffany often visited it and it was during this time that he was influenced by Ruskin and Morris.

Back in New York he decorated many houses for the new American rich but it was not until the late 1890's that he began to work with glass in a way which was to make him famous. In 1880 he patented *Favrile* glass, an iridescent technique made by exposing hot glass to a series of metallic fumes and oxides (see plates 13 and 61). Soon it was extremely popular and imitations were produced but never with Tiffany's unique flair and craftsmanship. He produced a vast amount of delicate, exotic and imaginative vases, glasses and

When Lilies of the day are done,
And sunk the golden westering sun.

lamps. In 1892 he exhibited a stained-glass window in Europe which guaranteed his influence and fame on the Continent and it was inevitable that the perceptive Samuel Bing should include Tiffany as one of his biggest exhibitors in his new shop. Despite many followers in America, Tiffany remained the only really original Art Nouveau artist in the decorative field that America produced.

But it was left to the architect Louis Sullivan to give American architecture a particularly Art Nouveau look. In the manner of Mackintosh he used light, simple assemblages of lines and curves. He worked with exposed cast iron and his decorative motifs were drawn from Celtic and Byzantine sources. The Bradly residence, completed in 1909, shows Japanese influences: flat areas, simple retilinear shapes and spaces. In this he had some influence on America's greatest architect, Frank Lloyd Wright.

Always out on a limb, individualistic and insular, it was inevitable that the Spanish creative spirit should produce its own brand of Art Nouveau, and produce it in a man of genius: Antoni Gaudí. The curving lines of his Parque Güell and the Casa Milá are waves of the sea arrested in movement, and waves moreover constructed out of a then revolutionary building material—concrete. His wrought-iron was, if anything, even more exotic, as the material lent itself to excess.

Gaudí's extraordinary imagination and strong religious leanings combined to produce his masterpiece, his unfinished Church of the Holy Family in Barcelona. He took full advantage of every architectural trick, every device of simulated movement, for confusing and exciting the eye. Obsessed and consumed by his passion he lived, at the end, a life almost of a hermit and it is sad that he had to leave his life's work incomplete.

Only one other architect ever came near to imitating him and that was the American architect Simon Rodia, himself an eccentric, who, in the 1920's, built a 'Pleasure Dome' or series of towers, constructed out of scrap steel, as fantastic as any spires by Gaudí Rodia even used Gaudí's device of embedding walls with broken tiles and pottery in a crazy, eye-confusing mosaic.

Themes in Art Nouveau

1

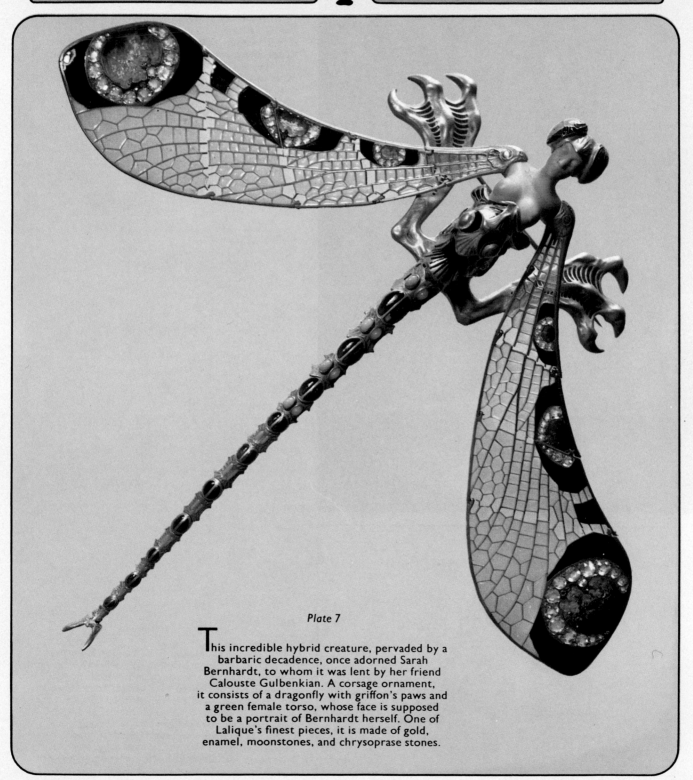

Plate 7

This incredible hybrid creature, pervaded by a barbaric decadence, once adorned Sarah Bernhardt, to whom it was lent by her friend Calouste Gulbenkian. A corsage ornament, it consists of a dragonfly with griffon's paws and a green female torso, whose face is supposed to be a portrait of Bernhardt herself. One of Lalique's finest pieces, it is made of gold, enamel, moonstones, and chrysoprase stones.

Plate 8

Honesty, a plant with purple flowers and transparent, fragile seed pods, was much beloved by Art Nouveau designers. The pods seemed to possess a fairy-like quality, and were often reproduced as in the example shown here. The pale greeny pods spiral up the side of a silver and gold vase produced at the Loezt factory.

Plate 9

This stained-glass window, bearing the title *Gather Ye Rosebuds*, uses the flower to great stylistic effect, together with a somewhat Pre-Raphaelite girl, sporting butterfly ornament on her sleeves. The window, by Alex Gascoyne, was made in 1906, and was described in *The Studio Book of Decorative Art* for that year as 'suggestive of wholly modern influences'.

8

10

Plate 10

This glass dragonfly by René Lalique is perhaps one of the most remarkable pieces he ever made. It is, in fact, a car mascot designed to be fastened to the bonnet by a bronze base, beneath which was attached a multicoloured lighted disc. Connected to the dynamo of the car, this disc revolved and cast rainbow shades through the insect. The faster the car travelled, the faster the colours changed. A truly fantastic and magical invention, outdoing Rolls-Royce's better-known flying maiden.

9

Plate 11

In this stained glass window entitled 'The Enchanted Wood' a peacock stands proudly on a wall surmounted by classical columns, beyond which may be seen the trees of the wood. Designed and executed by the Scottish artist Oscar Paterson, it has that fairy tale quality so often found in many designs of the period. In his windows Paterson specialized in modelling and etching glass with hydrofluoric acid. He often 'fixed' the enamel painting with a thin film of plain glass which, under heat, fused to the painted surface, thus forming a protection for it.

Plate 12

This breathtaking representation of the peacock, in gold, enamel, precious stones and opals, rivals anything created in pen and ink by Aubrey Beardsley. This corsage ornament by René Lalique is particularly interesting for the exquisite naturalistic rendering of the bird itself, contrasted to the highly stylized tail feathers which, with its 'eyes' dramatically picked out in opals, takes the form of a bow.

11

12

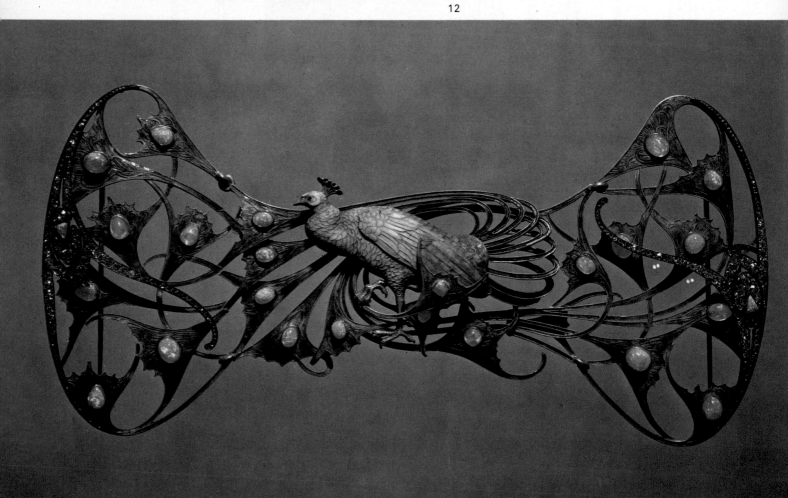

14

13

Plate 13

This classic vase made of *favrile* glass by Tiffany in 1902, displays another use of the peacock motif. The subtle 'eyes' weave gently up the sides of the vase, and the translucent blues and greens of the bird lend themselves to the properties of this particular type of glass.

Plate 14

This delicate pink vase is decorated by blue irises standing in relief. The effect was achieved by etching away the background with acid before applying the glaze. What could be a rather sickly colour combination has been cleverly avoided by the use of a rather severe, strong blue collar around the rim. The piece was made in France about 1900.

Plate 15

By the time Beardsley came to illustrate Oscar Wilde's *Salome* he was at the height of his creative genius. Much to the author's annoyance the illustrations themselves bear little relation to the actual story, which was used by Beardsley merely as a spring-board for his highly developed, decadent and exotic sense of design. One of the drawings is actually entitled *The Peacock Skirt*, while on the cover shown here, executed in 1907, he again uses the 'eyes' to achieve a fine effect in gold blocking on the green cloth binding.

15

Themes

Plate 16

The peacock became almost the symbol for the Art Nouveau movement, following the lead given by Whistler, as early as 1877, in his famous Peacock Room done in 1864. This bird with its exotic appearance, its iridescent colours, its elegant and sinister air, and above all the surrealistic 'eyes' in its tail, was used by Art Nouveau artists in every possible way. The bird on this glazed jug hangs its superb tail down the whole length of the form.

17   16

Plate 17

Throughout the ages candlesticks have lent themselves to every kind of decorative variation. The one shown here, by Jozen, was made for the *Salon des Beaux Arts*, and is in the form of a nymph, sitting upon a water-lily pad, sadly contemplating an iris in full bloom, thrusting its way out of the water.

Plate 18

The rose, a much used Art Nouveau motif, was particularly popular with Beardsley and with Mackintosh and his Scottish followers. One of these, Ann Macbeth, designed and embroidered this cushion cover. It has white roses in chain stitch, appliqué leaves, and a green linen border. During this period many such cushions, table-mats, table runners, and even collars and cuffs were embroidered with designs incorporating such stylized roses.

18

Architecture

2

Plate 19

This abstract window of coloured glass is one of many Gaudí designed for his small church of the Colonia Güell (1898–1914), in Barcelona. The Art Nouveau obsession with flowers is taken to its abstract ultimate: glowing, alive and vibrant, it owes little to Medieval origins.

Plate 20

Antoni Gaudí was fortunate in having as his patron a rich Spanish intellectual, Count Don Eusebio Güell, an enthusiastic Wagnerian and a strong Anglophile. For him Gaudí built an extraordinary palace in Barcelona, with cavernous rooms, enormous marble arches, twisting wrought iron, mushrooming brick columns, and mosaic chimney pieces. In the adjoining Parque Güell he created strange structures, including this curious, serpentine bench decorated with his favourite mosaic of tiles, pottery, shards, and pieces of marble, resembling the scaly body of a great snake or lizard.

Plate 21

Petrified waves of the sea; frozen sand dunes; every sea-form comes to mind when one looks at this extraordinary block of flats, the *Casa Milá*, built by Antoni Gaudí in Barcelona, between 1905 and 1910. The marine imagery is even carried out in the seaweed-like wrought-iron balconies and inside on the staircase balustrades. The whole building is as colourless as sand, while what appears to be a curving white band of solidified spray weaves along the roof. No less remarkable are the enormous chimney-pots, more like towers from some exotic fairy-tale than functional objects.

Plate 22

Deeply religious, Gaudí devoted most of his professional life to designing and building one of the most remarkable structures in the history of architecture, namely the Church of The Holy Family, Barcelona. It occupied him from 1909 until his death in 1926 and still remains unfinished. The whole building possesses the fantasy elements of a Hollywood extravaganza. It is all things: Gothic, high Art Nouveau, Expressionist, and Cubist. Rising from a Gothic base encrusted with marine-inspired convoluted forms, four huge hollow and pierced towers soar heavenwards. They resemble attenuated beehives, topped by tiled and convoluted spires which culminate in crosses like rochet wheels. The whole structure sprouts all sorts of gargoyles, including lizards, snakes, salamanders and snails.

20

Architecture

Plate 23

Unmistakably Art Nouveau in the organic and restless shape of the huge, bone-shaped windows and unconventional balconies, this elegant apartment house known as the *Casa Batlló* was built by Gaudí during 1905 to 1907. Inside none of the rooms is square, and the walls and ceilings appear to be in movement.

23

Plate 24

Designed as late as 1911, this curving staircase, from a house in the Avenue Mozart, Paris, with its sinuous wrought-iron stair rail, is representative of Hector Guimard's best work. He was responsible for the entire appearance of this hallway, including the lamp hangings and window frames. Similar ironwork by him was made for the Castel Béranger in Paris, which he began in 1894 and completed in 1898.

24

25

Plate 25

The Castel Béranger in Paris is one of Hector Guimard's most important architectural achievements. Every detail bears his stamp. Even the grills covering the vents have been carefully designed. Although the stonework here is more restrained, the wrought-iron gate embodies curved and straight lines, upright and horizontal forms, all caught in a cleverly realized tension, which is one of the characteristics of successful Art Nouveau.

Architecture

Plate 26

26A

April is the cruellest month, breeding lilacs out of the dead land.' So wrote T. S. Eliot. The dead pavements of Paris apparently bred green iron plants, burgeoning with buds, like mysterious overgrown cave-mouths. These are the famous Métro entrances, designed by Hector Guimard in 1900. Alas, not many of them are now left, but one has found its way to the Museum of Modern Art in New York. They show Guimard at his most fanciful, inspired by plant forms, utilized for a functional and mundane purpose.

B. An interesting view of one of the entrances from below: through a stained-glass window one can see the plant-inspired railing.

26B

Plate 27

Mackintosh's Glasgow School of Art stands out
as an important landmark in the history of
architecture, and Art Nouveau in particular.
Mackintosh, already a practising architect,
was successful in winning a competition for the
design, although contemporary Scottish opinion
considered that his conception was too advanced
for the time. The first part of the building
was erected between 1897 and 1899, while the
second part, the west façade of which is
shown here, contains the library and is
considered the more successful. It was built
between 1907 and 1909. Based on the Scottish
baronial style, Mackintosh added his own
version of attenuated bay windows. The low
doorway with its heavy architrave makes a
clever contrast to the soaring elegance of stone
and glass above.

27

Plate 28

The interior of the library repeats the soaring
lines of its windows. Tall square pillars of
stained pine rise seventeen feet from the floor to
carry a coffered ceiling. The construction of the
galleries was deliberately left exposed, as in a
medieval cathedral or church and in many
American Art Nouveau buildings. The narrow
supports, decorated with brightly coloured
facets, are in contrast to the bare main structural
columns. Mackintosh even designed the
bookcases, tables, chairs, and magazine racks,
leaving nothing untouched by his unique sense
of design.

28

Plate 29A, B

Mackintosh designed Hill House (A) in Helensburgh, Scotland, in 1902, for the publisher W. W. Blackie. One of many he designed, it is based on a traditional L-shaped plan, and reflects the traditional Scottish baronial style with its turrets, gable roofs, and small, rhythmically placed windows. Inside the house (B) he was able to carry out his usual scheme of organized space, white walls and delicate, attenuated furniture, subtly patterned in black and pastel colours.

29B

Architecture

Plate 30

This Paris doorway provides a first-class example of the French Art Nouveau style. In contrast to Mackintosh's sober, almost austere, designs, this is incredibly unrestrained and exotic. Asymmetric in conception, it is based on sinuous plant forms which sweep around the entrance, bursting into bloom above it.

Plate 31

This design for a music room was made by the English architect M. H. Baillie Scott in 1902. With Mackintosh he shared a preference for simple, straight lines, square forms and stencilled decoration. Its greens, pinks and yellows resemble a Post-Impressionist palette. Reflecting his interest in peasant art, it is in complete contrast to contemporary work being done in Paris and Barcelona. Baillie Scott was much admired in both Germany and Switzerland, and designed houses in Poland and Russia.

Plate 32

A *pièce de resistance* of Art Nouveau and of the Scottish movement, these white wood, stained-glass and leaded doors are all that are left of the famous Willow Tea Rooms in Sauchiehall Street, Glasgow, which Mackintosh designed for Miss Cranston, who must have been one of the most advanced of all 'tea shoppe' ladies. Carrying out the theme of the willow, Mackintosh deliberately attempted to convey the idea of a forest in the teashop by suggesting slender tree trunks in the use of white columns round the walls. These doors, apart from the skilful use of stained glass and lead, are remarkable for the fact that they are set in a narrow, unmoulded architrave.

Furniture

3

Plate 33

Perhaps the best known of all Art Nouveau objects, Tiffany lamps have become almost an interior decorator's cliché. At the time they were considered daring, and in dramatic contrast to the lamps of the period. This example is one of Tiffany's favourite tree forms, bearing green and purple fruit, set in a mosaic of vicious green and violet stained-glass leaves.

Plate 34

In strong contrast to the sort of desk that the turn-of-the-century well-to-do expected to have in his home or office, this one by Hector Guimard was made by him for his own house in Paris, in 1903. It curves; it twists; little of its decoration is symmetrical. Made of African and olive ashwood, in three shades of brown, it is very Japanese in feeling.

34

Plate 35

By an unknown English craftsman, and almost certainly from Liberty, this oak dresser, with copper fittings, is a beautiful example of the restrained yet decorative English style, owing much to William Morris and the Arts and Crafts movement. The ornaments are either English or French.

35

36

Plate 36

In marquetry and various woods this cabinet, by an anonymous French designer, displays the fanciful, erratic qualities often to be found in French Art Nouveau. Spindly brass fittings and motifs climb and grow over the surface like plants, and the soaring top shelf echoes, in a curved form, Mackmurdo's 'mortar board' tops. The vases and jugs in the cabinet are Italian and Hungarian.

Furniture

37

39

40

38

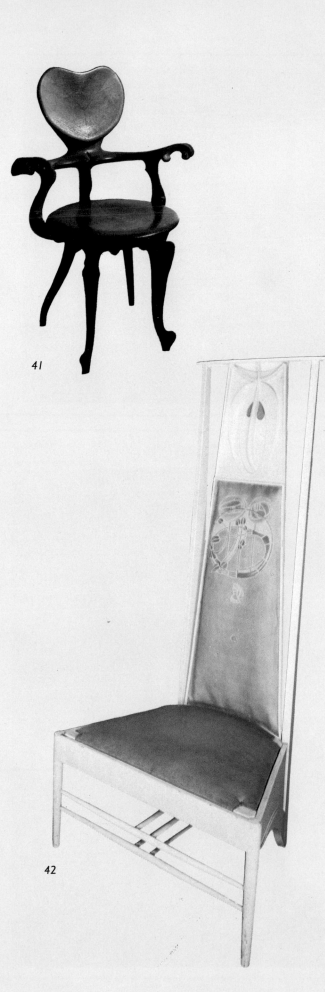

41

42

Plate 37

Strongly influenced by Mackmurdo, Charles Francis Annesley Voysey (1857–1941) was one of the leading architect-designers of the English Art Nouveau movement. He specialized in building small country houses based on Medieval traditional designs, which were reflected in the fabrics, wallpapers (see plate 2) and furniture he produced to go in them. Simple as it is, upholstered in leather and embossed with a cypher, this oak armchair betrays Medieval influence, as do the wallpaper and the carpet on which the chair stands, which are also by Voysey.

Plate 38

This graceful armchair by Louis Majorelle (1859–1926) was made in about 1900. It owes less to Majorelle's usual French classic inspiration than many of his pieces of furniture. One can sense the original impetus but the shapes, particularly those employed at the back of the chair, are pure Art Nouveau—as is the design on the fabric, which is a modern copy.

Plate 39

One of the most 'classical' of Art Nouveau designers, the German Richard Riemerschmid (1868–1957), eschewed the luxuriant flow and ripple of much Art Nouveau work. His ideas have strongly influenced furniture design up to the present day. This restrainedly elegant chair, made in oak and upholstered in leather, was made for the music room which he contributed to the Dresden Exhibition of Decorative Arts in 1899.

Plate 40

This settle and part of a panelled wall are all that is left of a music room designed by Carl Spindler and made by the cabinet maker J. J. Graf, both Austrians. Made of walnut with marquetry of pearwood, tulipwood, maple, amboyna and other woods, this settle was part of a prize-winning room carried out entirely in the same manner, for the Paris Exhibition of 1900. All the walls showed pastoral scenes in marquetry: the piano sported inlaid leaves; a table was comparatively simple and a glass-fronted cabinet echoed, in reverse form, the ogee shapes on the settle.

Plate 41

This chair by Antonio Gaudí is from a set of six which he made for the boardroom in the Casa Calvet, Barcelona. Bone-line and organic, it resembles driftwood rubbed smooth by endless tides.

Plate 42

This white, painted chair formed part of Charles and Margaret Mackintosh's contribution to the International Exhibition of Modern Decorative Art held in Turin in 1902. It came from the 'Rose Boudoir', one of the three rooms which formed the Scottish entry. The colours of the Rose Boudoir were of pearly lightness: white, pale rose, violet, green and blue.

Furniture

Plate 43

Although better known for his book designs and decorative work, Kolo Moser also turned his hand to furniture design. This cupboard is part of a suite made by him for a living room. Like so much Austrian work of this period, it is strongly influenced by Mackintosh, although the glittering and mosaic central panel reflects the style of the Austrian painter Gustav Klimt. Two portrait panels in bas-relief break up the starkness of the cupboard doors, while metal columns give to the whole a classic look.

43

Plate 44

Signed *Chez Gallé*, this worktable of carved ash, with marquetry and overlays of other woods, shows how Gallé decorated a simple form with highly stylized leaves and stems. Bearing the inscription, in French, 'Work is Joy' it demonstrates the designer's fondness for including moral or poetic phrases in his work.

Plate 45

This cabinet by Louis Majorelle, of about 1900, combines many woods: walnut and oak, coramandel and burr-walnut, all carved, curved, pierced and used as veneer. The picture on the panel at the top shows a seagull flying over a cliff, and the elaborate plant-shaped hinges are of wrought iron. This and the work table by Gallé (see plate 44) received much criticism when they were first exhibited in England.

Plate 46

Like so many Art Nouveau artists, George de Feure was interested in every aspect of design, and made this set of fittings for a suite of bedroom furniture. Finely conceived and modelled on plant forms, they are beautiful interpretations of utilitarian objects.

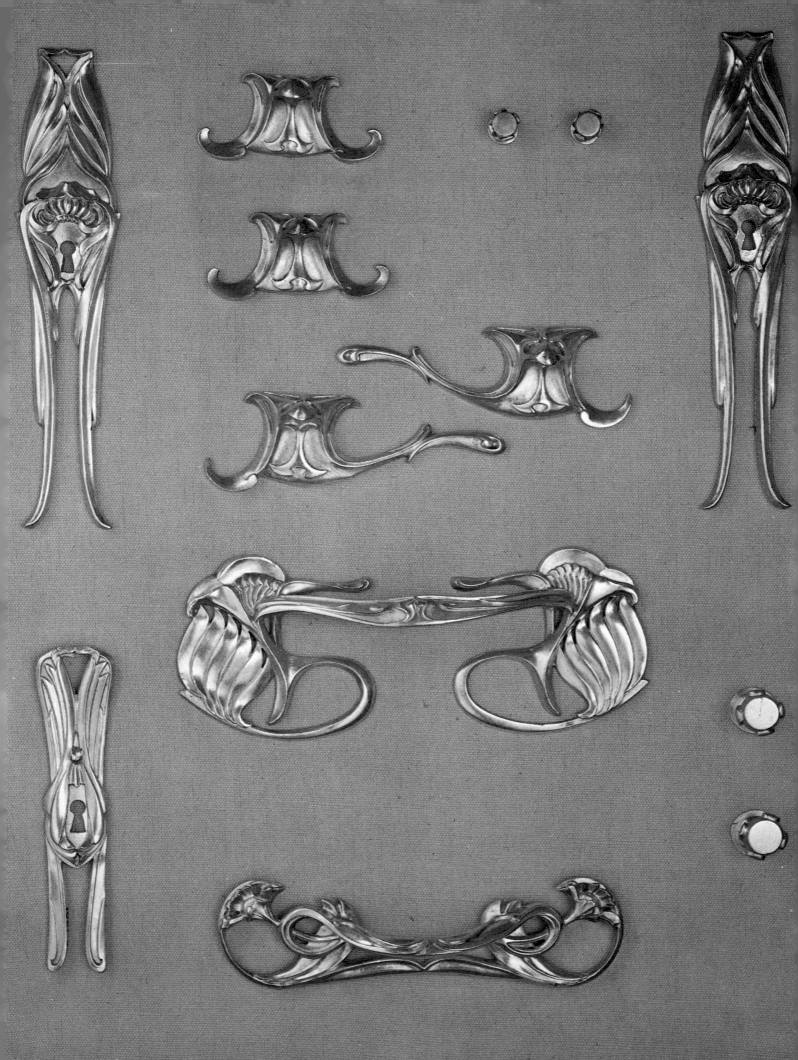

Furniture

Plate 47A, B

These two clocks display contrasting styles of
Art Nouveau. The superb bronze one (A) is,
surprisingly, unsigned, but is almost certainly
French. Phallic in shape, it is surmounted by the
head and shoulders of a woman bearing a
headdress of poppies, while its base is composed
of swirling leaves or drapery. The sombre
bronze is relieved by the turquoise centres of
the poppies. The gilded clock (B) has been
conceived in a marked asymmetrical form, and
although strongly curved it achieves perfect
balance. It is also unsigned, and is probably
French. A young girl and a cluster of irises
support the clock face, which is modern.

Plate 48

One of the first examples of the female form
being used as part of an electric lamp, this
bronze piece was designed by H. Beau in the
1890s. As a lamp it is not particularly successful,
the bulbs being too small and pale, as to be only
decorative adjuncts to the main purpose of the
exercise: that of displaying a woman and a
plant in a fanciful, fairy-tale manner. She rises
from the leaves, her feet peeping provocatively
through the foliage.

47A

47B

38

Furniture

Plate 49 A, B

Both these beautiful standing mirrors employ the sloped, converging lines so characteristic of Art Nouveau. But whereas the Continental mahogany one (A) is decorated with plant forms and a woman's head in pewter to give it interest, (B) relies entirely on its elegant lines, both straight and curved, to achieve a perfectly balanced effect. It shows the strong influence of Mackintosh, and may even be by him.

49A

49B

Ceramics

4

Plate 50

The story of the Goose Girl by the Brothers
Grimm was the inspiration for this vase made in
1900 by the Hungarian potter W. Zsolnay Pečs.
It is of grey earthenware, decorated in low relief,
and enhanced by a particularly beautiful
combination of coloured lustres. The whole piece
is mysterious and translucent, echoing the gold
and blue-green plummage of the peacock.

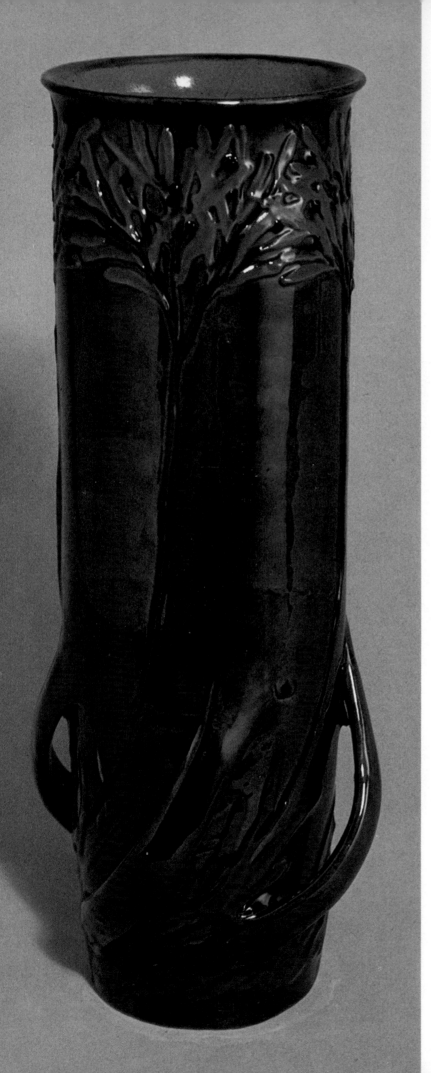

Plate 51

Bladderwrack seaweed forms the decoration on this highly glazed earthenware vase by Max Laeuger. Made in 1900, the low-placed 'handles' are characteristically Art Nouveau and add to the overall feeling of marine growth.

Plate 52

Wind-blown flowers bend around the sides of this vase created by Max Laeuger (1864–1952). Although he was primarily an architect he also specialized in ceramics. As with many artists in pottery at this time, he based his designs on Oriental patterns. This vase dating from 1898 is made of earthenware with relief slip decoration, and the whole covered with stained glazes. Laeuger exhibited in Munich in 1908 at the first Comprehensive Art Nouveau exhibition in Germany.

Ceramics

Plate 53

It was not only in the field of fine art that Art Nouveau found its expression; all manner of everyday items were designed and decorated in its style. Although appearing at first to be in the blue and white tradition of Chinese or Dutch porcelain, this English cheese dish bears an unmistakable Art Nouveau shape and decoration. The handle is particularly interesting, repeating the curling tendril design on the side.

Plate 54

In the decorative arts Holland did not produce much in the Art Nouveau style. One exception, however, was J. Jurriaan Kok, who worked for the Royal Rozenburg Porcelain works at The Hague. These subtly decorated eggshell porcelain pieces dated about 1901 have almost a Mackintosh flavour in their soft colours and display the fairy-tale aspect of Art Nouveau at its most pleasing.

Plate 55

These pieces from a tea and coffee service were designed by Henri van de Velde for the Royal Meissen factory. The decoration flows naturally and simply from the very forms themselves, giving a wholly satisfying result.

53

54

55

56

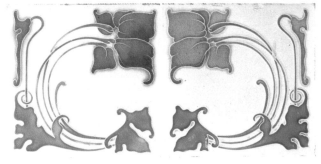

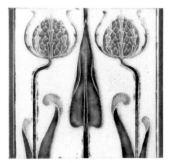

57

Plate 56

Possibly a paperweight, this hard porcelain plaque shows a skilful and lovely interpretation of a woman's head supported by oceanic motifs. It may have been one of a set portraying the elements. Ornamented with paste decoration and coloured glazes, it comes from the Sèvres factory and was made in 1901 by Taxile Doat.

Plate 57

There must still be in existence hundreds of fireplaces, bathrooms, hallways and staircases decorated with tiles bearing Art Nouveau motifs. Those shown here are typical, and were probably designed to make a frieze or a continuous upright panel.

Glass

5

Plate 58

This is a typical example of Emile Gallé's 'blown-moulded' glass, employing naturalistic raspberries in a wide range of yellows, reds and browns. In the technique employed a vase was first sculptured in wax, from which a mould was made. Molten glass was then blown into this mould and decorated with colour. All kinds of fruit lent themselves to this particular treatment.

59

60

Plate 59

This green and pink, two-handled vase, mottled with subtle water-drop-like blobs of gold was made by Johann Witeve Lötz. A follower of Tiffany, he ran a glass factory in Klostermuhle in Austria and worked from the late 1890's into the early years of this century. Like his master he was skilful in the use of iridescent effects as well as employing overlay and a cameo technique.

Plate 60

This exquisite glass figure made for the Daum factory, and modelled by Almeric Walter of Nancy in about 1902, embodies that mystery and veiled sensuality with which so many Art Nouveau artists endowed the female form. It is made of *paté de verre*, which is glass ground into a fine powder, mixed with liquid, usually plain water, and then baked in a mould.

Probably made in England, the unsigned myriad green glass vase trapped, as it were, in a cage of pewter tendrils which loop up to form two handles above the rim (A). Its broad treatment provides an interesting contrast to the slender, classically restrained, green glass vase supported on a bronze tripod (B), by the Austrian artist Professor Bakalowitz who worked for the firm of E. Bakalowitz and Sönne of Vienna.

61A

62

Plate 62

These two delicate vases made in 1902 in *favrile* glass, display Tiffany's particular contribution in the realms of iridescent technique. He was as much fascinated by this aspect as by the actual design. He noticed that glass buried for centuries acquired a glow due to erosion and exposure to mineral salts, and he succeeded in achieving this effect by mechanical means.

61B

Plate 63

This pitcher from the factory run by the Daum
brothers is considered one of their masterpieces.
It is entirely wheelcast, with an appliqué handle
and displays a fine harmony of softly blended
colours like a forest glade seen through an
autumn mist.

Fine Metalwork

6

Plate 64

Pewter plaques, usually displaying female and plant forms, were very representative of the period. On the centre of this dish a woman's head emerges from a lily pad.

65

Plate 65

This small and graceful dish employs an example of clothes forming an important part of the design. An early example of 'topless' dressing, the woman's body is beautifully modelled, as is the elegant curve of her head, adorned with pansies.

66

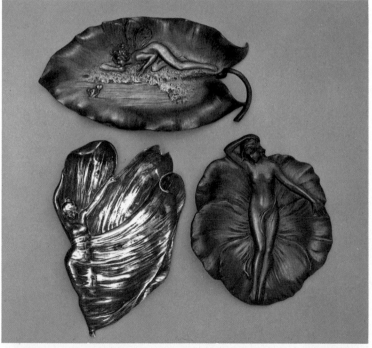

Plate 66

These elegant little dishes (the copper one is 16·5 cm long) all employ the female form in different ways. The two pewter ones also include naturalistic plant forms. The copper dish provides an interesting example of drapery being successfully used to form the main shape of the dish, and might well portray the Parisian dancer Löie Fuller. Such was the attention to detail typical of Art Nouveau that modelling of the woman's right arm and hand is carefully carried out on the underside of the dish. All these pieces display the fairy-tale aspect of Art Nouveau, and were probably mass-produced and exported from France.

67

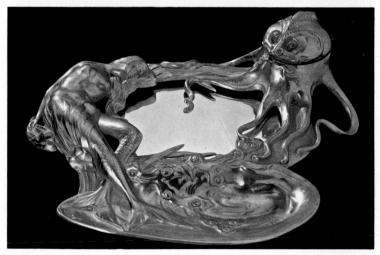

Plate 67

Perhaps one of the most strange and bizarre pieces ever conceived by an Art Nouveau artist is this silver-gilt inkstand, surrealistic in its conception, and embodying one of the favourite themes of Art Nouveau; that of the sea. The sleeping mermaid appears to be at the mercy of the menacing octopus, whose head forms the lid of the inkwell. Bladderwrack seaweed swirls around the water, which is simulated by a patch of mirror.

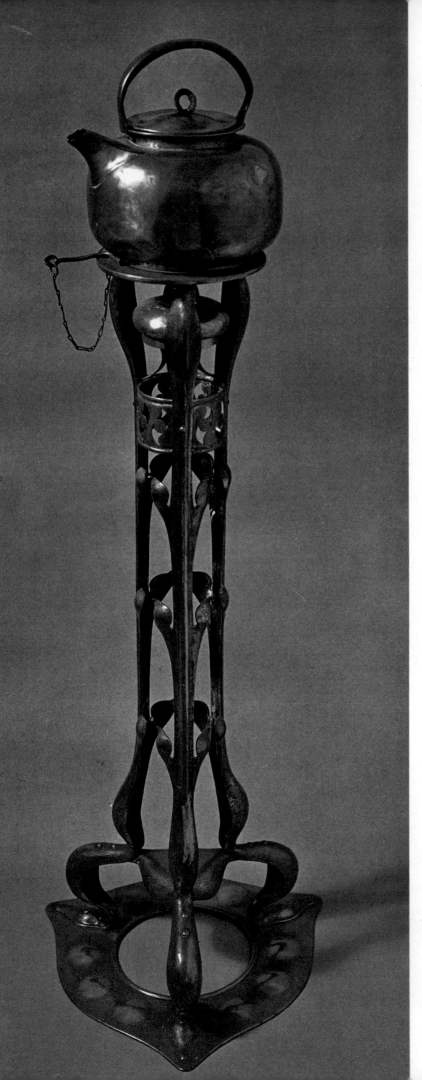

Plate 68

Most certainly made in France this unsigned pewter coffee-pot displays all the characteristics of French Art Nouveau. These may be seen in the asymmetric swirls in the handle and lid knob, and in the symmetric leaf and phallic shape in the surface decoration.

Plate 69

Here a traditionally shaped copper kettle stands on a tall, fanciful pedestal, also of copper, beaten and given Art Nouveau curves and piercings. It is English and was made by Reynolds.

70

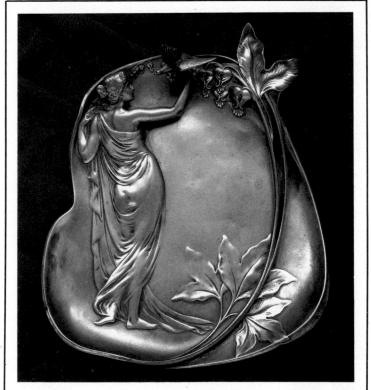

71

Plate 70

Charles Robert Ashbee (1863–1942), although principally an architect, produced some of the most interesting and characteristically Art Nouveau silver. This bowl, typical of his work, was made in 1893. It is embossed and chased with leaves, and has cast legs. It was made by the Guild of Handicraft, which Ashbee founded in 1888.

Plate 71

This wall plaque shows a standing woman sculpted in low relief, while the bird alighting on her hand is modelled completely in the round. Such wall plaques were exported from France under the name *Articles de Paris*.

Fine Metalwork

72

Plate 72

These five picture frames clearly illustrate the diverse styles possible within one art form. (Top left) This beaten copper frame inset with mother-of-pearl shows the influence of Mackintosh, and may be an actual piece from his school. (Top right) A moulded frame, the panels on either side are occupied by typical Art Nouveau women, hovering over water lilies. Their arms, holding a garland, stretch across the top of the frame. (Middle) Silver frames such as this, inset with blue-green enamel, were very popular at this time and were often decorated with entwined and overlapping forms. (Bottom left) Brass flowers and stems encircle this frame which, in spite of its symmetry, appears to undulate and flow as if alive. (Bottom right) This severely designed frame, made of brass, was obviously inspired by Egyptian designs.

Plate 73

Nothing could be further removed from the fanciful leaf spoons than this cutlery place setting by the Vienna Sezessionist, Josef Hoffmann. Not only do they reveal the very strong influence of Mackintosh, but they are curiously modern, even timeless, in their design.

Plate 74

A striking transformation of natural forms into everyday articles is revealed in these beautiful silver-gilt spoons. The handles, in the form of delicate branches, terminate in leaf-shaped shallow bowls through which run a mass of fine veins. Although unsigned they are very like the work produced by Prince Bogdar Karagerovevitch, a specialist in the design of silverware.

73

Jewellery

7

Plate 75

Splashed with a splendid sickness, the sickness of the pearl.' So wrote the English writer G. K. Chesterton; and this phrase accurately sums up the decadent, *fin de siècle*, aspects of Art Nouveau. Nowhere is it more beautifully realized than in this brooch by Lalique. The baroque (or misshapen) pearl hangs beneath the brooding and mysterious face of a woman, carved out of crystal, wearing a headdress of purply-black flowers upon her flowing black hair, whose tresses gather round her.

Plate 76

This brooch, by Feuillâtre, reflects the escapist attitude of *fin de siècle* Society, with the delicate, remote profile of the girl, the fairy headdress of butterflies wings and antennae, beautifully modelled in gold filigree, and set with moonstones. Made in France in 1900, it is contemporary with Tinkabell, the fairy in J. M. Barrie's famous play *Peter Pan*.

Plate 77

It is, perhaps, in jewellery that Art Nouveau found its most beautiful and successful expression, and one of its greatest exponents was René Lalique. This centre panel for a choker or dog-collar is one of his finest pieces. It displays a daring and exciting combination of colours as well as being finely executed. The face is carved on chrysoprase (a precious stone of the quartz family) while the hair is chiselled gold.

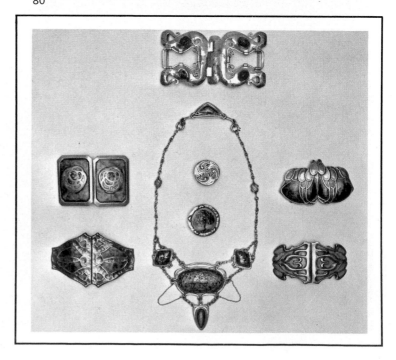

Plate 78

Typical of the obsession with plant and insect forms, this brooch displays a bee poised on a convolvulus flower. It is made of gold and *plique à jour*—translucent enamels—and was made in 1901 by C. Dessosiers for Fouquet.

Plate 79

Lalique's mastery of material and form is well displayed in this matching hair ornament and buckle. This set is made of horn, gilded metal, and is inset with carved glass and topaz.

Plate 80

Two of the favourite materials used by Art Nouveau artists working in jewellery were silver and enamel, particularly peacock blue enamel.

Plate 81

One of the most magnificent pieces of jewellery designed by Lalique, this necklace or jewelled collar epitomizes the spirit of Art Nouveau. It is constructed from nine enamel-on-gold panels, linked together by filigree gold mounts, each supporting a round Australian opal.

Painting and Sculpture

8

Plate 82

This dashing example of Art Nouveau painting by the Royal Academician Sir Herbert Herkomer, was painted in 1898. Entitled *Day*, and in its flowing gilt frame, it tells us much about the *fin de siècle* spirit in England. Unlike Klimt's women, the completely nude figure here seems cold and passionless, and represents an ideal and acceptable English interpretation of the female form. On the other hand the trees and landscape appear, like the frame designed by the artist, wild and painterly.

Plate 83

Auguste Rodin (1840–1917), whose work has been described as both neo-Baroque and Romantic, shares with many Art Nouveau artists, in spite of his unique surface treatment, the same fluidity of line and the tendency to suggest some hidden meaning. This small group, *The Secret*, reflects the Art Nouveau influences of the period. He strongly influenced Minne with his sense of movement, though his personal sensuality was foreign to the other sculptor.

84

Plate 84

The subject of this painting by Johannes Thorn Prikker (1868–1932), entitled *The Bride* and executed in 1892, is perhaps a nun taking the veil, enveloped in a garment decorated with white flowers that take on the shape of skulls. She is linked to the figure of Christ hanging on the cross by her garland of myrrh, which becomes, round his head, the crown of thorns. In the foreground phallic tulips appear to reach forward to engulf her, while in the background a group of candles burn, their pale flames reaching up into the vaulting. The artist has used cool blues, mauves, lilac and gold, to blend the whole scene together.

Painting and Sculpture

Plate 85

Samuel Bing, who founded the first Art Nouveau shop in Paris in 1889, commissioned the young Frank Brangwyn (1867–1956) to cover the whole shop facade, in the rue de Provence, with murals. 180 feet long, they were painted on canvas and mounted on to the building. He also executed similar works for the entrance hall, of which *Music*, shown here, is one.

Plate 86

The idea that man and nature, even if in conflict, are one, pervades much of Art Nouveau work. In this religious painting *The Chosen One*, the Swiss painter Ferdinand Hodler (1853–1918) shows the infant Christ, surrounded by angels, kneeling before a small sapling. It was specially executed for Henri van de Velde's Hohenhof, in Vienna.

Plate 87

Between 1905 and 1911, Josef Hoffmann built the Palais Stoclet in Brussels. Too dramatic for a private house and more Cubist than Art Nouveau, it nevertheless contains mosaic murals by Gustav Klimt which are perhaps his masterpiece, consisting of highly stylized trees punctuated by single or embracing figures. This drawing is a detail of a cartoon for one of the women.

85

86 87

Painting and Sculpture

Plate 88

Sarah Bernhardt, known as 'the Divine Sarah', was a great patron of the Art Nouveau movement. René Lalique made jewellery for her, Alphonse Mucha and Eugene Grasset created posters, while this bronze statuette depicting her in the title role of Rostand's drama *The Princess Lointaine*, is by Marius Vallet.

Plate 89

Unhappy in love, Munch's view of women was pessimistic. He felt that, like vampires, they would devour him. In this painting, *The Dance of Life*, completed in 1900, the young man in the foreground dancing with the girl in the flowing red dress, symbolizing passion, is watched over anxiously by two women, one in white, symbolizing youth and purity, the other in black, signifying death. The whole scene is redolent of the oppressive *fin de siècle* spirit.

Plate 90

A star of the Folies Bergère, Löie Fuller, whose famous scarf dance caused a sensation, as she whirled and spun like a top, was the embodiment, even a symbol, of the Art Nouveau spirit. This exquisite bronze figure of her, after a model by Agathon Lèonard, is called *Le jeu de l'Echarpe*, and is dated about 1900.

89

Painting and Sculpture

Plate 91

This anonymous bust by an Austrian sculptor is of Daphne: cool and remote, beautifully modelled and serene, very much in the manner of Sappho

Plate 92

The epitome of Art Nouveau—the feminine form, plant form and translucent colours; all are here in this bronze and enamel bust by the French artist Godet. The plant from which the woman emerges, and the petals round her head, even resemble the veins and markings of butterflies so that the whole exquisite rendering suggests fragility as well as solidity.

Plate 93

Sappho, the great classical Greek writer in the seventh century BC, gathered around her a group of women interested in music and poetry. In this terracotta bust by S. Obiolo, her temples are adorned with pale poppies, while her thick hair falls upon her breasts, both draped and revealed by a green shawl drawn about her shoulders.

91

92

93

66

ART DECO

BY DAN KLEIN

INTRODUCTION

*'In olden days a glimpse of stocking was looked on as
something shocking, but now God knows anything goes'*
Cole Porter

ETHEL MERMAN sang this Cole Porter song in 1934,
and the refrain mirrors a frenzied world recovering from
the crippling effects of one war and speeding towards
another. "Anything goes" is a catch-phrase that neatly
captures the spirit of Art Deco, the name that is now
fast becoming a household word to describe every
kind of decorative design between the wars. It has the
advantage of being a convenient international term
differing only in pronunciation from country to country,
but it can lead to endless confusion as it covers so many
schools of design. Both a carved sycamore chair by
Paul Follot, romantically decorated with flowers and
fruit, and a chaise longue by Le Corbusier with a
chromium-plated steel tube frame can pass for Art
Deco. It is merely the loosest coat-hanger word coined
after an exhibition held in Paris in 1966 called 'Les
Années '25'; that exhibition concentrated on the
'twenties and the famous 1925 Paris 'Exposition Inter-
nationale des Arts Décoratifs et Industriels Modernes'. In
1969 Studio Vista published Bevis Hillier's book, 'Art
Deco', and in 1971 the Minneapolis Institute of Arts
organized an exhibition called 'The World of Art Deco',
which included decorative design of the 'thirties. Now
for better or worse we are stuck with the term; it is meant
to evoke a panorama of flat-chested flappers dancing
the Charleston in the latest cocktail dresses from Paris,
of interior decoration smothered with floral patterns, of
the geometry of Odeon cinemas, or of chrome and
glass furniture. Some sorting out is necessary before
the images become too confused and kaleidoscopic.

The designers working between the wars can be
divided into two broad categories; the sybarites who
covered every available surface with their new stylized
flowers and fruit, and the revolutionaries who wanted
purity of line uncluttered by decoration and who
turned to the aesthetics of machinery for inspiration.
The first group, consisted mainly of Paris fashion designers and interior decorators, extravagantly led by Paul
Poiret, the second revolved around the various avant-
guarde schools of architecture and their leaders, and

in particular the Swiss-born architect, philosopher and
designer, Le Corbusier, who claimed that a house
should be a "machine for living in". But one concept
was common to all Art Deco designers, that of total
design. Whether you wished your house to look like
clockwork or like an exotic jungle, every detail from
the keyhole to the radiator grille was worthy of the
designer's attention. This has greatly affected the sur-
vival rate of complete Art Deco buildings. Some of the
most important Art Deco design went into the building
of factories, but the enormous changes in the world of
industry have made it impossible to preserve them. On
the other hand, with such attention to every sort of
design, a great many items of interest remain, and the
hunt for Art Deco is never ending.

*'So we came to the Ritz Hotel and the Ritz Hotel is devine.
Because when a girl can sit in a delightful bar and have
delicious champagne cocktails and look at all the important
French people in Paris, I think it is devine, I mean when a
girl can sit there and look at the Dolly Sisters . . . . .'*
Anita Loos – Gentlemen Prefer Blondes

PARIS led the world of fashion during the 1920s, and as
the Art Deco movement was largely initiated and inspired by fashion designers, all eyes turned to Paris for
the '1920s look'. From 1915 till 1925 Paul Poiret was the
undisputed dictator not only of what women should
wear, but also of the decor that would best complement
the clothes he designed. His colours and designs were
strongly influenced by Diaghilev's Ballets Russes, and
in looking for a beginning to Art Deco most art historians
agree that the movement was born in 1909, when that
year Diaghilev brought his Russian dance company to
Paris for the first time. The explosion of colour and the
boldness of design that the Parisians saw during that
season brought an end to the delicate tendrils and
curves of the Art Nouveau period. Flowers became
formalized and geometric; perhaps the clearest
example of the transition from whiplash tendrils to
geometric rosebuds can be seen in the designs of
Charles Rennie Mackintosh, the Scottish architect,
painter and designer, who stripped Art Nouveau design

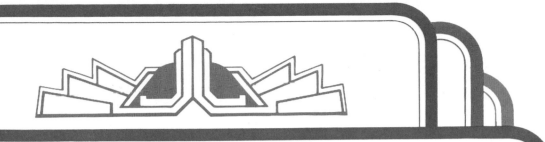

of gratuitous ornament and pointed the way to the cleaner lines of Art Deco. There were other favourite Art Deco motifs besides the flower; for instance fountains, leaping gazelles and, as geometry took over, sunbursts and lightning ziggurats. The discovery of Tutankhamen's tomb in 1923 made the Egyptian influence predominant for a while. By the 'thirties the geometrical shapes that had made animals, flowers and plants look angular gained the upper hand and became decorations in themselves; a "brave new world of unforeseen technological advance" made the aesthetics of machinery fashionable and pure geometry became the decorative mania of the 'thirties. In amongst all this, traces of Fauvism, Cubism, Futurism or Negro art were to be found. Art Deco designers borrowed freely; they made decorative use of every new invention but were rarely innovators themselves. Rather was the movement led by "fashion stylists, graphics designers, craftsmen or theorists whose prime concern was with taste and style rather than with practicality and performance".

'Take a tuck in that skirt Isabel, it's 1925'
Anita Loos

FOR a while the novelty of Art Deco lay in the fact that it was dominated by the designers of the fashion world. There were various reasons for this, perhaps the most important being that during the 'twenties fashion became big business; a wider market was made possible by greatly improved communications throughout the world. Even Poiret, the king of 'haute-couture', lectured on the advantages of mass-production and the joys of ready-to-wear dresses. These clothes were worn by a new type of woman who emerged after World War I with the new-found independence she had won by working while the men were away at the front fighting. Poiret helped her to express her freedom by freeing her from the corset and completely changing her shape; his dictates were taken seriously, and the latest dress-style was of the greatest importance. Fashion designers exploited women's weakness for new clothes by changing styles and colours as often as possible; there was talk of fever-chart hemlines as dress lengths shot up and down. Waistlines travelled too, from below the bust to below the navel. But certain things stand out as distinguishing marks of the Art Deco period, such as cloche hats, bandeaux worn immediately above the eyebrows, short cropped hair (which became softer, slightly longer and more wavy in the 'thirties), 'cupid's bow' mouths and the complete disappearance of the bust. Certain colours, too, evoke the 'twenties and 'thirties, like tango (a burnt orange shade that took its name from the popular tea dance), silver and black.

Just as important as the clothes were the accessories, perfumes and make-up that accompanied them. Poiret set the fashion by marketing his own perfume; Jeanne Lanvin, Chanel, Coty and Worth followed suit. The women's magazines published articles re-assuring their readers (particularly unmarried women) that make-up, if discreetly used, was not sinful. Modernist dressing-tables became the focal point of the bedroom, a new sort of shrine to beauty. Great care was taken over the packaging of cosmetics, particularly perfumes, and the best glass designers like Baccarat and Lalique were employed to design scent bottles. Lalique also designed

a face powder box for Coty. Jewellery was either very expensive from Cartier, Boucheron or van Cleef & Arpels, or unashamedly false. Chromium and the newly invented bakelite (which was made in a variety of splendid colours) were used for costume jewellery; the more exclusive pieces were couturier designed, but much of it was simply mass-produced. Bakelite was considered exotic enough to be used with precious stones and precious metals even by Cartier. Brightly coloured enamels in jazzy designs were also very popular, and some of the enamelled cigarette cases, powder compacts, buckles and brooches of that period were beautifully designed and have become collectors' items today. And in true Art Deco style, even accessories like handbags, scarves and shoes paid the greatest possible attention to decorative brilliance.

'Poor child! Her little cartier diamond bracelet flashed in the sunlight as she released the brake of her car and, as she sped away, I thought 'clever Noel Coward' Poor little rich girl indeed'
Angus Wilson – For Whom The Cloche Tolls

POOR Little Rich Girl! In America she was called "the flapper", in Italy "La Maschietta", in France "La Garçonne".

However you described her, she set the mood for the 'twenties. "The free and easy boy girl with shingled hair, a cigarette, a driving licence." Mrs Pankhurst and the suffragettes had started the fight to liberate women and World War I accelerated their emancipation. They began working in jobs that had hitherto been filled exclusively by men and began to make their mark in the business world, particularly the business of interior decoration, fashion and decorative art. Many of the famous designers in Europe, America and England were women. There had been women designers in the Art Nouveau movement, but they were far less involved in the commercial aspect; apart from anything else Art Nouveau was an arts and crafts movement that deplored the machine; Art Deco used the newest possible machinery to make good craftsmanship available to the general public. It was a case of supply and demand, for new fortunes had been acquired during World War I and the re-distribution of wealth brought forward a large clientele with new tastes and a new type of home to furnish. The richest of the 'nouveaux riches' had plenty of money to spend, but many of them did not trust their own taste. After the war they found themselves with money but no position in society; 'Studio' magazine referred to them as "the present possessors of great

wealth . . . . a different and on the whole less cultured class". Many members of this new moneyed class were starting from scratch. They wished to achieve a total new look that concealed humble beginnings, and the best way was often to employ the services of an interior decorator. A few people were willing to spend vast sums of money on their homes and a few designers, like Emile-Jacques Ruhlmann, catered for their needs. Ruhlmann's furniture was the height of luxury, "veneers of rare woods, amaranthe, violet-wood, macassar ebony, encrusted with ivories and materials like morocco leather and sharkskin". His 'Pavillon d'un Collectionneur' at the 1925 Paris Exhibition won the highest praise and admiration, and today his furniture is to be found in museums and important private collections. But Ruhlmann was something of an exception and the costly workmanship that went into his furniture a hangover from a bygone age.

The new middle class wanted elegant homes that were easy to run – sumptuous mansions with liveried servants belonged to another era. Modern chic made a completely new set of demands on designers and decorators. Households were becoming smaller, but everything in the home had to be a witness to taste and style. As space became more limited, every bit became a vital living area. Kitchens were no longer confined to dark basements staffed with cooks and maids. Self-respecting citizens spent time in them and it was important that they should be pleasantly designed and practical. Bathrooms took on a completely new look, with streamlined fittings and new labour-saving floor and wall coverings in jazzy designs. No decorative detail was free from comment or criticism in fashion journals and magazines devoted to interior decoration.

As entertaining became more of a problem, formal dinner parties gave way to cocktail parties; a whole new society cult was born and of course the clothes, accessories and furniture to go with it. Modernist cocktail cabinets were given pride of place; cocktail accessories became as ridiculous as the small-talk that accompanied these new drinks. Asprey made a cocktail shaker in the shape of a dumb bell; Ronson made a monkey lighter and cigarette dispenser combined – at the touch of a lever an Art Deco monkey bends over to pick up a cigarette out of a metal container. Kitsch was in its element at the cocktail bar.

'I designed innumerable dresses and coats, accessories such as hats, head-dresses, gloves, shoes, muffs, fans and masks and many other objects for interior decoration, chairs, screens, light-fittings, cushions, vases, what have I not designed. Even bath-towels'
Erté

THE ever increasing ranks of the middle classes were preoccupied with taste and kept designers busy. They considered it safer to invest in the proven design talents of others to decorate their homes than to be branded as tasteless. Poiret attracted the richest if not the classiest members of society to his gardens and salons with his 'masked balls of Neronian pomp'. The balls were meant as more than pure entertainment; they were a shop window for Poiret's exuberant tastes, and significant because they were designed specifically to show off the decorative arts, which the general public were only too anxious to buy for themselves. Poiret also formed a design studio known as L'Atelier Martine, in 1911. For a while Raoul Dufy collaborated with him over this and Poiret made use of other first-class, though as yet unknown artists. The studio was chiefly for the production of carpets and hand-woven or hand-printed textiles. As a commercial venture it failed (partly because Dufy left), but it set the fashion for design studios.

Industrialists began to appreciate the value of good design, and the big department stores in Paris, realizing the business potential of interior decoration, employed famous designers to open departments for them. Louis Sue and André Mare started the Compagnie des Arts, which provided well-designed furniture at reasonable prices; Paul Follot worked for Bon Marché; Marcel Dufrène for Galleries Lafayette, and at Printemps there was L'Atelier Primavera. All these workshops prided themselves on having a distinctive style and competed with each other for excellence of design. Other European capitals followed the example set by Paris. London was slowest of all, and it was only after a decade of complaints by enlightened writers in 'Studio' magazine:

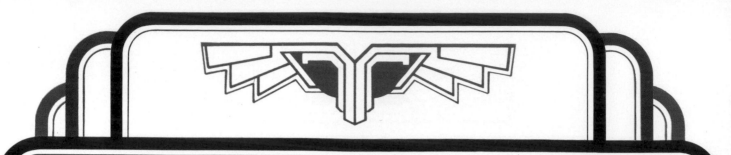

("it is unfortunate that the patterns displayed in most of the shops are so extraordinarily dull and commonplace," 'Studio', 1924) that Waring and Gillow went modern with a department for French furniture under the direction of Serge Chermayeff. The best English furniture in the 'twenties and 'thirties was that sold at Heal's, some of it designed by Sir Ambrose Heal; but excellent as it was, this belonged more in spirit to the Arts and Crafts movement of earlier decades. It was not till the very late 'twenties and early 'thirties that English interior decoration developed a recognizable and interesting style. In America there was plenty of money, particularly before the Wall Street crash in 1929, but according to Paul Frankl (remembered best for his 'skyscraper furniture') the general public was quite unconscious of the fact that modern art had been extended into the field of business and industry. Frankl wrote: "The only reason why America was not represented in Paris 1925 was because we found we had no decorative art". By 1929 this was no longer true with sumptuously furnished

buildings like Radio City Music Hall where Donald Deskey was responsible for the sheer fantasy of every aspect of interior decoration, or William van Alen's glittering Chrysler building, or the Chanin building with Jacques Delamarre's amazing radiator grilles, elevator doors, theatre on the 52nd floor and friezes in Atlantic terracotta and bronze adorning the outside of the building. Interior decorators opened up offices in New York and were kept extremely busy. It was a profession which many of the newly emancipated women considered suitable and not too shocking. The best known of American lady designers, Elsie de Wolfe, had designed the Colony Club as early as 1905, and was later commissioned by Frick to decorate an entire floor of his 5th Avenue mansion. In England and America Syrie Maugham, the wife of the author, excited comment with her white interiors but was criticized for going too far when she coated valuable Georgian furniture in white paint to tone in with her schemes. Interior decoration became big business and there was much money to be made from it.

'While painting in the Salon D'Automne makes no advance . . . . while sculpture remains where it is . . . . decorative art continues its sure progress and captivates visitors' interest. It is only receiving its just due. Without any doubt decorative art is harvesting the fruits of experience and it is mainly of cubism that we are thinking, formerly only cultivated in the realms of pure and disinterested art. Now it is the 'Modern Man's Office', which holds the attention of the exhibitors and designers: another time the 'Private Cocktail Bar', 'The Dining Room' or 'The Living Room'.'
Studio Magazine, 1931

THERE were two important developments which affected living accommodation after World War I. First of all, with smaller apartments, every bit of space was valuable and had to be carefully designed. Then there was the important link between art and industry, which opened up a whole new field for designers. Factories were no longer a blot on the landscape with chimneys belching smoke. Where possible the ugly mechanics of production were hidden behind streamlined façades, as for instance in the Hoover building at Perivale, just outside London. Executive

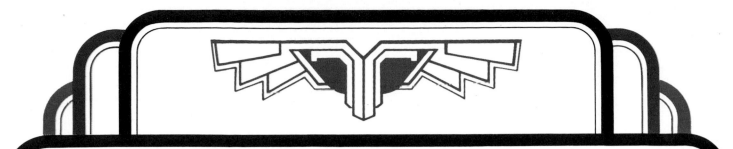

offices had to flatter the taste and personality of the executives using them and interior decorators were called in to create a suitably impressive look. In the home, kitchens and bathrooms became the decorator's new playground; technological advance was complemented wherever possible by the designer's creative talents. Particular attention was paid to lighting, and new inventions like radios or electric fires took on the craziest disguises. One of the illustrations in this book shows a sailing-ship fire, another a radio in a lacquered 'chinoiserie' case. As far as lighting was concerned, there was an endless variety of chandeliers, wall fittings and decorative lamps; some showing off the amazing skills of glass manufacturers like Lalique or Argy Rousseau, some the superb metalwork of Edgar Brandt or Majorelle. The most functional of objects became decorative.

It has not been possible in a short book to include illustrations of the work of all the great designers of the 'twenties and 'thirties. For instance there is no illustration of Puiforcat's silver, of Sonia Delaunay's textiles, of Rosenthal porcelain or of Décorchemont 'pâte de verre' glass. On the other hand there are illustrations by lesser craftsmen or designers, because a great part of the charm of Art Deco lies in unimportant ephemeral items like the 'Savoy Cocktail Book' or a mass-produced plastic inkwell. Many of the illustrations show the work of English designers, partly because it was easily accessible but mainly because the restrained English Deco look has been eclipsed by the flashy French look and has not yet had the appreciation it deserves.

'Since a poster is a way of addressing a hurried passer-by,
already harrassed by a jumble of images of every kind,
it must provoke surprise, rape his sensibility and mark his
memory with an indelible print'
Posters & their Designers –
Studio Special Number, 1924

SPEED and publicity were the two important aspects of the modern world of the 'twenties. Cars, aeroplanes, trains and travel were in the news, and on the artist's mind. Both Le Corbusier and Ruhlmann made attempts at designing cars. Yvonne Brunhammer in her book on Art Deco sees the aeroplane and the automobile designed "in new forms taken over from cubism and its successors". Travel was the subject of many decorative panels (like the painted ceiling in the lobby of the Chrysler building). Ocean liners became floating museums, particularly the 'Ile de France' and the 'Normandie' where the interior decoration was done by a distinguished team of craftsmen and designers; on the 'Normandie' (launched in 1932) the main dining room had walls lined with hammered glass panels and two gigantic chandeliers by Lalique; the lounge had four decorative panels by Dupas, and there was furniture by Ruhlmann in some of the better suites. The French government encouraged such extravagance as being the best possible publicity for the luxury arts and crafts, and money invested in publicity during the 'twenties and 'thirties was considered well spent.

Improved communications opened up undreamed-of export markets; people moved faster and further than ever before and it became increasingly important to advertise. In a special number of the 'Studio' in 1924 devoted entirely to advertising, the editor says: "This is the day of the poster. Some of the best brains in the business world of today are concentrated on the possibilities of the poster as a means for advancing trade and the services of the most skilful artists are requisitioned to forward the desired end," – artists like McKnight Kauffer and Frank Brangwyn in England, Cassandre and Jean Dupas in France, Van Dongen in Holland. In England the railway companies (including London Transport) commissioned some of the best posters, with "instantaneous appeal, and the story truthfully stated in language so simple that the real meaning cannot be misconstrued". The 1924 'Studio' special poster number concludes: "Poster designers are producing some of the most outstanding work of our time." These designers worked not only on posters, but on advertisements in magazines, on wrappers, labels, booklets, prospectuses, and letter headings.

'Studio' brought out another special number in 1925 devoted to Art and Publicity and here the editor appraises the importance of advertising: "The old days have passed, and with them have gone the old-time manufacturers, merchants and tradesmen who lived and worked on their own premises, the craftsmen and

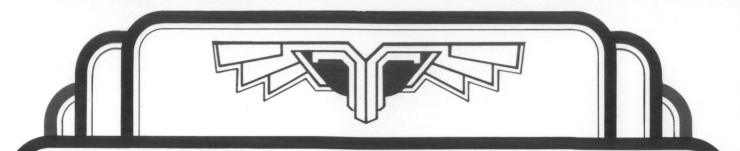

prentices, and the travellers who journeyed by coach; the conditions they knew have long ceased to be and have crumbled before the forward march of progress, production on a huge scale, collective bargaining, the coming of the large store, the rise of the trade unions, and business activities embracing the whole world. Nowhere have the effects of this transformation been more apparent than in the direction of advertising and printing. Printed advertising has advanced with the times, and in recent years to so marked a degree, that it now occupies a higher place in everyday affairs then it has ever reached before." Although the benefits of advertising were universally agreed upon, there were still complaints that businessmen too frequently failed to appreciate the value of good design and failed to realise that "such homely subjects as bacon, eggs, syrup, shirts and socks or glue" could acquire new glamour in the hands of a good artist. But there were a few firms that believed in using artistic talents to promote their merchandise, firms like Bon Marché in Paris, Wesson Oil in America, or Eastman Dyers and Cleaners in England. Their advertisements are admired forty years after they were done and continue to influence poster art and graphic design today.

'The great life of the machine has shaken Society, has snapped all chains, opened all doors, and cast its eyes in every direction'
Le Corbusier

SO far most of the decorators and designers mentioned have been those who catered for middle-class tastes and the middle-brow intellect; these artists and craftsmen asked no searching questions about social reform, nor did they concern themselves with the deeper implications of changes in modern society. Not so Le Corbusier, whose all-white pavilion at Expo '25 was meant as a protest against the surfeit of prettiness on display in other pavilions. The pavilion was called 'L'Esprit Nouveau' and did all it could to break with tradition and to bend people's minds towards a modern way of life and a new aesthetic. Le Corbusier was a severe critic of the 1925 Exhibition and made his protest in strong terms. "We protest in the name of everything. In the name of happiness and well-being, in the name

of good taste . . . . . it is said that decoration is necessary to our existence. Let us correct that. Art is necessary to us, that is to say, it is a disinterested passion which elevates us." These words stab straight at the heart of Art Deco, the art of decorating and ornamenting every available surface. Le Corbusier was not alone in his attack. Many other schools in Europe combined philosophy and architecture and deeply mistrusted the attempts of the 'nouveaux riches' at building over-decorated fortresses to shut out the problems of the real world.

In Holland Van Doesburg edited the forward-looking magazine 'De Stijl' from 1917 to 1931; he and his followers were interested in finding forms to express the newness of twentieth-century experience, "to construct without any illusion, without any decoration, is one of the principal aims of the Stijl movement". Perhaps the most compact expression of the ideals of this school is to be found in a wooden chair by Rietveld. It is an amazing 'construction' preoccupied with the arrangement of material in space, an experiment to express philosophy in a chair. The result looks most uncomfortable, but this was no easy-chair designed to cosset the rich. The chair was meant to keep the sitter "physically and mentally toned up".

In Germany Walter Gropius had established the Bauhaus a few months after the end of World War I. During the fourteen years of its existence, intellectuals, artists and craftsmen (Gropius, Klee, Breuer, Feininger, Kandinsky, Moholy-Nagy) fought with and against each other to express their own brand of modernism.

In Italy the Futurist movement under the leadership of the poet Marinetti published manifesto after manifesto in high-flown rhetoric. "There is no more beauty except in strife. No masterpiece without aggressiveness . . . . . we shall sing of the great crowds in the excitement of labour, pleasure and rebellion; of the multi-coloured and polyphonic surf of revolutions in modern capital cities; of the nocturnal vibrations of arsenals and work-shops beneath their violent electric moons; of greedy stations swallowing smoking snakes; of factories suspended from the clouds by their strings of smoke; of bridges leaping like gymnasts . . . . of broad-chested locomotives prancing the rails like huge steel horses

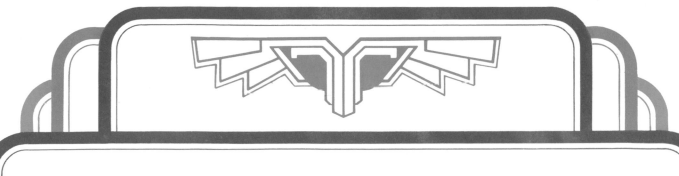

.... and of the gliding flight of aeroplanes, the sound of whose screws is like the flapping of flags and the applause of an enthusiastic crowd." This 'cri de coeur' seems far removed from the happy exuberance of Paul Poiret and the unquestioning fun of Paris fashion. Although the ideals expressed by these various schools seem a long way away from the gentle art of decoration, it is important to mention them in a book about Art Deco. Le Corbusier, Marinetti and Van Doesburg were working at the same time as Lalique, Ruhlmann, Poiret or Sonia Delaunay. The work of the philosopher artists helps to put the work of the fashion designers and interior decorators into perspective. Moreover, although Art Deco designers had neither the time nor the inclination to stop and listen to the impassioned outbursts of the moderns, the evolution of their style owed a lot to the innovators in the enemy camp. After the Paris Exhibition of 1925 the rash of ornamentation subsided and decorative art became simpler. Aldous Huxley in his "Notes on Decoration" published in 'Studio' Magazine in 1930 sums up the fusion of opposing elements: "The contemporary style has evolved out of the harsh artistic puritanism of a cubism which, in its first violent reaction against the prettinesses would suffer nothing but straight lines and angles, into something more ripe and humane . . . . whether we like it or not, we have actually grown to prefer the simplicities. We have tempered them, however, with a certain graciousness of form."

'Cocktails and laughter but what comes after?'
Noel Coward

WHEN did Art Deco end? Why did it end? What followed it? There isn't really any answer to these questions – Art Deco was never a specific movement. Futurism began and ended with Marinetti; De Stijl died with Van Doesburg, but decorative art muddled its way through thick and thin. In a sense it has never ended; it merely progressed on a tortuous route changing its look every now and again when a new designer came along, and a new trend was set. Some authors have made Art Deco end with the Wall Street crash in 1929. Certainly

there were great changes after that; depression was in the air, but in some cases this led to a show of extravagance for appearance's sake (one thinks of luxury skyscrapers standing half empty during the Depression – the Empire State building was renamed the Empty State Building). However, the simplicity of the 'thirties design did not really signify hard times; as Aldous Huxley said in the 'Studio' 1930: "Simplicity of form contrasts at the present time with richness of materials and has invented many new materials to work on. Modern simplicities are rich and sumptuous; we are Quakers whose severely cut clothes are made of damask and cloth of silver." In 1933 Donald Deskey, who designed the interior of Radio City Music Hall, wrote: "From the chaotic situation arising out of an era of prosperity without precedent for decoration, produced by Expo '25 in Paris.... a style emerged... one lot of motives was simply substituted for another ... ornamental syntax consisted almost entirely of a few motifs such as the zigzag, the triangle, fawn-like curves and designs". Between the wars changes in ornamental syntax occurred with great frequency, which made for an enormous variety of styles, but also makes the task of defining Art Deco a very difficult one. Art Deco is a thousand different styles, the ever changing look of the decorative arts of the 'twenties and 'thirties. The illustrations that follow can only serve as an introduction to a vast area of design, decoration, ornamentation and fantasy.

SYMBOLS AND SHAPES

musique

ABOVE
Chrome and glass table-lamp with gilded spelter lady. Although this is a mass-produced object, it is charmingly designed and well made. By the 1920s the wonders of electricity were taken for granted, designers found light-fittings a new and inspiring challenge. Lights had either to be completely hidden or be made decorative. We find everything from streamlined chrome, poised dancing ladies in porcelain, bronze or spelter, condemned like lost souls in Hades to support globes of light until the glass got smashed or the ladies were put away in cupboards by a new generation who found them vulgar.

TOP RIGHT
It is generally agreed that American Indian art and particularly the stepped shape of Aztec temples had a considerable influence

on design in the 'twenties. This is particularly noticeable in some skyscrapers of the period (for instance the Empire State Building in New York), in furniture design, "even in things as unsacred as radio-sets" (Bevis Hillier – 'The World of Art Deco'). The above illustration shows two scent bottles, ordinary mass-produced objects whose shape must surely have been inspired by American Indian pyramids, or tombs of Old Mexico.

ABOVE
Small desk or table watch by Meyrowitz (of London and New York) in silver gilt and enamel; the numerals are unmistakably '20s as is the green sun-ray enamelling on the face of the watch, but the stongest part of the designs is in the scarab-wing sides showing Egyptian influence. After Tutankhamen's tomb was discovered in 1923 Egyptian motifs appeared in designs of every sort: one of the best examples was in Graumann's

Egyptian Theater on Hollywood Boulevard where the stage "made King Tut's tomb look like the old family burial vault".

RIGHT
Ziggurats, cubes, geometric flowers and leaves, silver, all the symbols and signs of French Art Deco here combine to make a glorious silk evening scarf. Nothing is known about the designer or manufacturer, but the sheer extravagance and assurance of design suggest one of the Paris fashion houses. Paris fashion had no conscience about borrowing from an art movement or from the work of a particular painter whose colour palette or design might translate successfully into fabric. Motifs from the Ballets Russes, from Cubism or from the Fauve painters all found their way into fashion design. Also during the 'twenties painters were commissioned to design for fashion houses.

ABOVE

Design by Léon Bakst for the costume of Potiphar's wife in the ballet "La Légende de Joseph", for which the music was by Richard Strauss. Léon Bakst (1886 – 1924) was the chief designer for Diaghilev's Ballets Russes when this company gave its first season in Paris in 1909. With their costumes and scenery, Bakst and his collaborators brought about a revolution in the history of scenic art, which in turn revolutionized Paris fashion, introducing a new colour spectrum, new shapes, a completely new look. Paul Poiret introduced this look into the Paris fashion world; the new colours had liberated him from "an atmosphere of 18th century refinement", and he says "Now I have let some wolves into the sheepfold, those lively reds, greens, purples and blues make all the rest sit up".

LEFT

This soup tureen comes from a dinner service by Spode called 'Royal Jasmine' and dates from the 1930s. The sparse geometry of the decoration shows a complete reaction against the busy flowers and festoons that were among the more popular motifs of the 'twenties. Clean lines, partly inspired by the cubist painters, partly by Le Corbusier's purist philosophy of design were used for decoration. Basic shapes (like the square, the triangle and the circle) and their spatial arrangements greatly interested the designers of the 'thirties. Silver, cream and apple-green were colours that were very much in vogue for interior decoration.

PREVIOUS PAGE

'Miss Modern' of the early 1930s would be wearing one of the new 'tailored frocks' perhaps trimmed with chromium buttons (the latest thing in 'smart notions'), a bangle (worn above the elbow with a handkerchief slipped through it) and a necklace in chromium and bakelite might complete the outfit. There were novelty necklaces of all sorts from "ordinary common or garden tap washers with big marble-like beads in any gay colour as a contrast – whoever could guess – ?" to the most sophisticated Bauhaus-inspired all-aluminium jewellery. It was a comparative novelty that all this jewellery was unashamedly 'false'. The dancing figure from which the necklaces are hung is by the Austrian sculptor Lorenzl.

LEFT

Detail of a very long paste, jade and silver necklace and pendant, probably French and dating from the mid-'twenties. Long strings of beads were a vital fashion accessory in the 'twenties and went well with the flat-fronted look. This is a more dressy and infinitely more expensive version of the long dangling necklace and meant for evening wear. The links are beautifully articulated so as to follow the line and movement of the body. The necklace would come down to about the navel of a woman of average height. Paste and diamanté settings came very much back into fashion during the 'twenties, but one rarely finds a piece as superbly made as this.

BELOW

Wallpaper by Donald Deskey in the second mezzanine men's lounge of Radio City Music Hall, New York. The theme depicted is "Nicotine"; the paper is printed in tobacco brown on aluminium foil paper. The American designer Donald Deskey was in charge of the overall interior decoration of Radio City Music Hall, and designed much of the splendid furniture and many of the accessories that help to turn it into the 'Art Deco' monument that it is today. The building was designed by Rockefeller Center Inc. architects, and it was they who chose Deskey to assist in the furnishing and decoration of the building.

RIGHT

Two of a set of six fashion plates for the Parisian Furrier Simon Frères. With artists such as Poiret and Erté doing fashion designs, fashion drawing became a highly cultivated art. Erté designed for 'La Gazette du bon ton', for 'Vogue', and was associated regularly with 'Harper's Bazaar' for 22 years. The designs illustrated are probably from around 1929. Martin Battersby in 'The Decorative Twenties' describes the fashion in that winter: "small and head-hugging hats were worn with the huge fur collars, collars which often continued as a border round the hem of the coat which was invariably three-quarter length". The greyhound seems almost to have become a fashion accessory during the 1920s.

BELOW RIGHT

A collection of clips and buckles, some in bakelite and some enamelled. Belt buckles and clips came under the heading of 'utility jewellery', they were immensely popular, and as the term suggests, very useful. An issue of 'Woman's Own' in the early 'thirties devotes an entire article to clips. A clip could be worn in a beret, "but that doesn't mean it won't look equally well in a simple felt hat, clipped a little to the left of the centre front of the band. Again, if you had two they'd be the perfect finish to a pair of plain satin shoes for your evening frock. As for the really lovely effect on a black chiffon velvet evening-bag – well, words couldn't describe it!"

TOP
Hand-printed silk with bold design where hot shades of red and purple fight with subtler blues and pinks. The fabric is probably French, the design slightly reminiscent of Léger and his machine aesthetic, the colours still inspired by the Ballets Russes. Diaghilev's ballet had a profound effect on Paul Poiret who dictated fashion for a decade after World War I; it was he who encouraged artists to design textiles. Some of the most striking fabrics of all were designed by Sonia Delaunay whose work was characterized by hard geometric shapes in bold primary colours. Her fabrics were exported far and wide and became famous when film stars started using them for their wardrobes. The 'coat of many colours' she designed for Gloria Swanson is by now as legendry as Joseph's.

ABOVE
Four scent bottles in the shape of a bow-tie made by Baccarat for Guerlain of Paris. They contained a perfume called Dawamesk. It is typical of the period that a masculine design was used for an essentially feminine object. The pyjama suit or an exact copy of a man's dinner-jacket was fashionable evening wear for the flapper and this takeover of masculine fashion even found its way into toilet accessories. During the 'twenties packaging received almost as much attention as the merchandise, especially where cosmetics and perfume were concerned. Baccarat, Lalique (who designed for Coty) and Sabino are a few of the most famous glass makers who designed scent bottles, probably causing the bottle to cost as much as the scent itself.

RIGHT
Detail from a carpet in wool and chenille designed by Frank Brangwyn and made by James Templeton & Co. of Glasgow (c 1930). A pamphlet advertising the carpet says: "when an artist of the worldwide eminence of Mr Brangwyn can collaborate successfully with manufacturers, 'Art in Industry' is no longer an aspiration but a reality". Brangwyn designed furniture (for Pollard), tableware (for Doulton) and glass (for James Powell). The intention was to design good furniture for British homes at ordinary prices, "to design for the limitations of machinery, and yet produce a thing of use and beauty" ('Studio' December 1930).

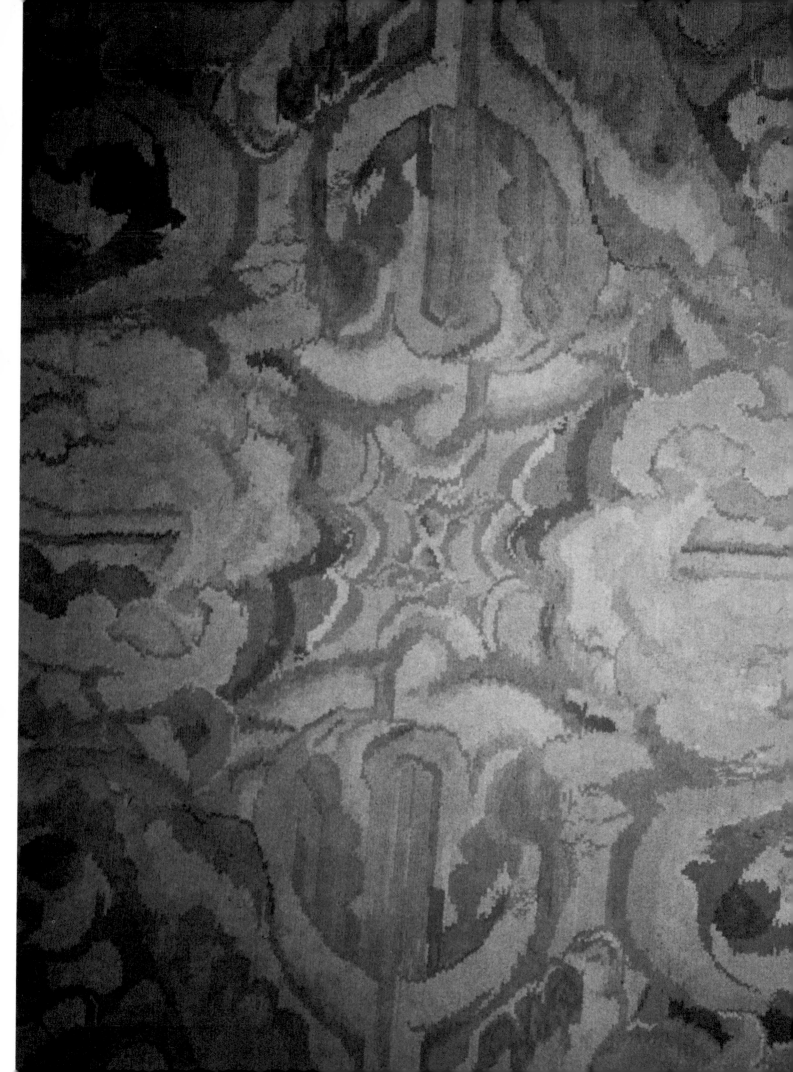

Drop earrings in jade, onyx and diamonds by Boucheron of Paris. With the shorter hair styles of the 'twenties and 'thirties, long earrings became a very popular form of jewellery, whether made of precious stones, paste or plastic. Van Cleef and Arpels, Cartier and Boucheron were probably the three most famous jewellers of the time and catered for the mood of wealth and extravagance of the 'twenties. During the 'thirties fortunes dwindled and jewellery became severer and simpler in design. Dress-clips (designed to fit together and make a brooch), earrings and bracelets were the most fashionable accessories.

Superb platinum, onyx and diamond pendant with a real pearl. Signed by the French jeweller Lacloche. Onyx and diamonds worked together were very much the traditional jewellery of the 'twenties. During that decade great progress was

made in cutting diamonds and George Fouquet, in an article on modern jewellery in the May 1930 'Studio' says "The novelty for 1929 lies in the completely white note. But how new is this white stone jewellery and how much it differs from the old! Progress has been made in working on the diamond – pieces are composed and carried out which consists of a mixture of brilliants and brilliants cut in the form of wands, triangles, or any other form, allowing the artist to obtain from diamonds whatever effect he chooses."

ABOVE
A pen and water-colour drawing done on silk, which illustrated the mid-'twenties look. Dresses fell in a straight line from the shoulder, the bust had virtually disappeared and the waist had moved down to the hips. Hair was worn bobbed or shingled which brought earrings back into fashion. Long hair was not fashionable as it could not be concealed under cloche hats.

Hemlines varied in length from season to season: ladies' legs had after all only been on show in public since after the end of World War I and couturiers had difficulty in deciding how much leg should be shown.

RIGHT
French and English bags and shoes from the mid-'twenties. The maroon leather shoes are French. At the back is a black moiré silk evening bag by Cartier, with a decorative buddha in jade and the letter 'C' in emeralds; the green morocco bag decorated with twisted leather strips is by Finnigans of Bond Street, London. It is not known who made the other two bags. Most bags were small during the 'twenties. For day wear they were usually made of leather with chrome or plastic decorations (during the 'thirties there were elaborately designed handbags made entirely of plastic); for evening wear small embroidered or beaded bags were fashionable.

Dressing table and stool combined; English c 1930. By the 1920s the sanctimonious approach to the bedroom had disappeared and it was not necessary to be too serious about designing bedroom suites. There were many ingenious designs for dressing tables; some had huge circular mirrors with low shelves on either side and there were many variations of the table and stool combined. The Parisian firm of Saddier produced some of the best of these. Light fittings were often incorporated into the design, usually vertical neon tubes set into jazzy chromium fittings. The dressing table became a glorified shrine to cosmetics and fashion.

BELOW

Powder compacts, powder boxes and cigarette cases. The round glass box is by Lalique who also designed the box decorated with powder puffs for Coty (used by them until very recently). Powder was sold loose and beauty specialists recommended it be applied with fur puffs. "Do not wipe powder on, dust it on: women who 'wipe' powder on their faces use the wrong method," says an advertisement for washable, fadeless hygienic 'I'vajack puffs' in 1933. All women carried a flap-jack compact in their handbags. If you could not afford a gold compact encrusted with diamonds and rubies from Cartier, the next best thing was a compact with a jazzy enamelled design (and there were hundreds to choose from). No handbag was complete without some sort of flap-jack, which was of course changed to match the bag.

RIGHT

Three pieces of jewellery by Jean Fouquet. At the top, a ring in platinum, onyx and diamonds; in the middle, a brooch in coral, diamonds and onyx; and at the bottom, another brooch in platinum, diamonds and onyx. These pieces have a mid-'twenties feel to them, before jewellery started going ultra-modern. Jean Fouquet was one of the most original jewellery designers of the 'Deco' period; his later pieces became more geometric than those illustrated here and looks as if it is based on designs lifted straight from French cubist still-life paintings. He very much liked using precious stones combined with bakelite and plastic.

FURNITURE

The bronze is by the Hungarian sculptor Keleti; the wrought-iron mirror and the commode with a design of drooping foliage are probably of French origin; the two vases with geometric patterns in brightly coloured enamels are by Faure. The process of enamelling over glass was a popular one during the 'twenties and practised by many of the French glass designers, but none of them achieved the boldness of pattern or brilliance of colour attained by Faure. Most of his pieces are now in museums and private collections.

RIGHT
A decorative screen designed by Frank Brangwyn and sold by the Rowley Gallery, London. Many artists designed decorative panels and screens during the 'twenties and 'thirties though it is rare to find one in inlaid wood. Lacquer work came back into fashion and was more usual for this type of decoration. There were several artists who specialized in this work; perhaps the best known was Jean Dunand whose most famous screen was one 22 feet high and 27 feet across designed for the smoking-room of the transatlantic liner 'Normandie'. Eileen Gray, an English designer working in Paris, was another artist whose lacquer screens were superbly made and beautifully designed.

RIGHT
Table by Emile-Jacques Ruhlmann especially designed for the Yardley premises in Old Bond Street. The table is in Macassar ebony and brass bound at the foot. Ruhlmann in conjunction with Reco Capey designed a complete scheme for Yardleys in the early 'thirties at the very end of his life. He died in 1933 after a lifetime's reputation as one of the greatest of French decorators. He was only interested in designing for the richest collectors and his furniture made no concessions to the growing demand for artist-designed pieces at commercial prices. He used the rarest woods and infinite work and craftsmanship went into every piece. His 'Pavillon d'un Collectionneur' was one of the highlights of the 1925 Paris Exhibition.

93

TOP LEFT
Blonde wood bureau and drawers with brass handles and panels of antelope skin; on gilded base with scroll-like decoration. The use of antelope skin has a touch of surrealism about it, though it is not as pronounced as Schiaparelli's sofa in the shape of lips or her hat in the shape of a shoe. It is difficult to suggest any maker for this piece of furniture. Furniture varied greatly in order to suit the whim of a particular decorator or client, and no material was considered too impractical. There were some favourites (sharkskin, lacquer, glass or aluminium, for instance), but every designer fought for originality of style, and was eager to find new and untried materials to work in.

LEFT
English peach mirror glass table by James Clark Ltd c. 1935. White and coloured mirror glass and mirror furniture was very fashionable during the 'thirties. With improved manufacturing techniques glass became more flexible and more varied. There were mirror glass cocktail cabinets, desks and clocks and the English designer Oliver Hill even designed a dangerous sounding glass chaise longue supported by four glass balls, (though this was intended primarily for exhibition purposes). Oliver Hill was also responsible in collaboration with Lady Mount Temple for a spectacular bathroom in which walls, ceiling and all fitments were grey mirror glass, and the bath and basin lined in gold mosaic.

FAR LEFT
Two 1930s electric fires, one in the shape of a sailing-boat, the sails acting both as reflectors and heat conductors; the other a modernist design in polished chrome. There were several variations on the sailing-boat fire, one of the commonest being a butterfly electric fire. As with lighters and radios, designers could give free reign to their

fantasies when it came to modern household equipment for which there was no real precedent. It was a refreshing aspect of design between the wars that a light-hearted joke was perfectly acceptable if the finished object was practical and well thought out.

BELOW LEFT
Dressing table, stool and mirror by the American designer Paul Frankl, who wrote in his work 'Form and Reform' published in 1930: "Ornament = crime. Here is the axiom of extreme modernism." American interior design did not begin to go modern until 1930 or slightly before. There were plenty of American interior decorators during the 1920s but more often than not they tried to capture a European feel in interiors they designed. An all Spanish, or all Italianate, or all French Empire room was what they were after more than the all modern look. American Modernism did not really catch on till the 'thirties.

LEFT
The bronze and ivory figure of a lady with two greyhounds is by Chiparus. The delicate 1920s lady's writing desk has a matt crackled polish overlaid with stylized painted flower and fruit decoration. The decoration is typically French, probably of the period between 1918 and 1925. It is reminiscent of the work of Paul Follot or André Mare, both of whom used flower and fruit in characteristically Art Deco designs, and it might perhaps come from the workshops of one of the big stores in Paris where these designers worked. Follot was responsible for the workshop at the Bon Marché, and Mare in conjunction with Sue founded the Compagnie des Arts Français as early as 1919.

ABOVE
Display cabinet in dark wood with ivory inlay by Paul Follot. This cabinet was shown at the 1925 Paris Exhibition. The flower and leaf decoration running down the central dividing strip is typical of this designer who catered for enlightened middle-brow taste. His furniture, whilst incorporating Art Deco design, stuck to fairly traditional shapes and ideas. This was partly due to the fact that he had to design with the general public in mind, as from 1923 onwards he was head of the decorating department at one of the largest Paris department stores, Bon Marché.

ABOVE RIGHT
Mirror and cabinet by Carlo Bugatti. Not very much is known about Bugatti – he lived through both the Art Nouveau and Art Deco periods and exhibited at the famous Turin Exhibition in 1902. His style was completely individual, with a strong oriental influence. His furniture tends to be impractical (for example his huge uncomfortable chairs), but every piece displays a superb sense of craftsmanship. The cabinet above is beautifully inlaid with metal and brass, the mirror is leather painted with a floral design. Bugatti's designs bridge the gap between Art Nouveau and Art Deco, between romanticism to geometry. The bronze and ivory figure on the cabinet is by Chiparus.

RIGHT
French side-cupboard with Chiparus bronze and ivory figure of a dancing lady and above that a pair of wall bracket lights by René Lalique. Although he was over 60 years old at the beginning of the 1920s, Lalique's output was enormous and he was the sole designer of the glassware produced by the firm. His son helped him with the economic and productional aspects of the business and the work exhibited by the firm at the Paris International Exhibition of 1925 brought world-wide recognition. Lalique experimented in the field of illuminated glass and design pieces that were meant primarily as decorative ornaments rather than sources of light.

LEFT
Weighing-machine, chair and table at Radio City Music Hall, New York; the chair and table are by Deskey. This remarkable "height weight metre" is shaped like a skyscraper – a typical piece of 1930s American 'modernism' Paul Frankl, who was famous for his skyscraper bookcases and display cabinets, said of the American skyscraper: "We had our skyscrapers and at that very date (1925) they had been developed to such an extent that, if it had been possible to have sent an entire building abroad, it would have been a more vital contribution in the field of modern art than all the things done in Europe added together."

BELOW
Dining table by René Lalique made in c1931. Only a few of these tables were made – the top is one thick sheet of opalescent glass, supported by four glass columns on a solid glass base, the whole held together by a framework of chromium-plated metal. Lalique's output was so vast and varied that it would have been possible to acquire a complete dinner service made by the firm including menu holders and candelabra. Lighting could be from one of his beautiful decorative lamps or glass wall brackets. Only food and cutlery might upset the scheme.

INTERIOR DESIGN

PREVIOUS PAGE
I.S. Chanin's bathroom in the executive suite of the Chanin building on Lexington Avenue and 42nd street, New York. The building was completed in 1929. The interior decoration was by Jacques Delamarre under the supervision of I.S. Chanin (head of the Chanin Construction Company Inc.). This bathroom in the sky, on the 52nd floor of the skyscraper block, is decorated with cream and gold tiles; the small frieze of ceramic bird tiles above the bath conceals a ventilating duct. The shower and basin taps, the rims of the heavy engraved glass shower doors and the sun burst pattern above these doors are all gold-plated. A splendid example of the extravagance and splendour of American 'Modernism'.

BELOW
A corner of Roxy's private suite in Radio City Music Hall, with furniture and lighting by Donald Deskey. S. L. Rothafel, known better, or almost exclusively as Roxy, was the genius behind this fantastic music hall, theatre and cinema combined with its 36 precision dancing Rockettes, its vast stage and incredible foyers and lounges fitted with carpets, wallpapers, furniture, murals, chandeliers, bronzework and statuary, all executed by artists of the modern school. Leading American artists were commissioned to lend their talents to the decorative scheme. The most modern materials were used wherever possible: aluminium, cork, bakelite and formica; pyroxalin-coated fabric; structural mirrors and glass walls; honeyskin, tweed, pigskin and patent-leather upholstery and furniture of chrome-plated steel and tube aluminium.

RIGHT
A detail of the entrance hall to the Daily Express Building, Fleet Street, London (1931). The architect responsible for designing the entrance hall was Robert Atkinson. Serge Chermayeff, writing in the 'Architectural Review' for July 1932, describes it as "a mass of fibrous plaster, gilded and silvered in the tinsel manner, suggesting a provincial picture palace". John Betjeman, writing 40 years later calls it "a fabulous Art Deco entrance hall, with wonderful rippling confections of metal". On the exterior of the building black strips of glass set in chromium curve around the corner on which it stands, giving a marvellous effect of modernism and streamlining.

Part of the foyer at the Savoy Theatre, London, showing the ceiling, a decorative urn, and one of the radiator grilles designed by Basil Ionides, who redecorated the theatre in 1929. This designer was responsible for some of the best interior design in London during the 'twenties and early 'thirties, including work at the Savoy Hotel, Claridge's and Swan and Edgar's. In an article on Interior Design in 'Studio' Magazine for May 1929, Ionides wrote: "Simplicity is of course the note to be aimed at today, and also good colours. The day of the elaborate plaster ceiling is gone and its place is taken by simple stepping or coffering."

RIGHT
Replicas of Edgar Brandt's wrought-iron and bronze decorative panels. The originals were made in 1922 or 1923; the replicas were made to decorate the interiors of the lifts at Selfridge's when the Oxford Street store was rebuilt in the 'twenties. Recently the lifts were modernized and the panels given to various museums in England. One is constantly amazed how Brandt could hammer and coax iron into such delicate shapes, full of expression and movement. However intricate his work, whether it be a radiator grille, a lamp, a decorative panel, or a piece of furniture, it always achieves a superb balance between practicability and decoration.

RIGHT
A recently converted 1930s style bedroom. Although not authentic in every detail, the curving mirror strips, the tubular steel and plate glass of the shelves behind the bed, the furniture, the objects and the light fittings by Lalique give a distinct feeling of the 'thirties to the room. There has been a great revival of interest in design between the wars brought about by important exhibitions such as 'Les Années '25' at the Musée de l'Art Moderne in Paris in 1966 and the Minneapolis exhibition in 1970. It has affected and inspired designers in the early 1970s most noticeably in the graphic arts, with lettering and art-work of the 'twenties and 'thirties appearing frequently in advertising features and on posters.

LEFT

Anteroom to Claridge's ballroom, Brook Street, London. Claridge's was re-decorated in 1929 under the supervision of Basil Ionides, and became a showcase for the work of some of the best English designers and interior decorators; the new ballroom was designed by Oswald P. Milne with a series of decorative panels by George Sheringham; the carpets were by Marion Dorn. The greatest effort has been made to preserve this extravagent decoration – when stair carpets wear out new ones are woven to the old design. The Causerie, the main lobby, the restaurant, the ballroom, the bedrooms and the bathrooms all retain the splendour of the 'twenties as far as possible.

BELOW LEFT

Elevator doors in the lobby of the First National City Trust Co., originally the City Bank Farmers Trust Co. in the Wall Street district of New York. The building was put up in 1931. The elevator doors are of monel, a mixture of nickel and brass. It was high speed elevators (together with American steel-frame construction) that made skyscrapers possible, and one of the most important features in determining the success of an office building was the speed, efficiency and comfort of the elevators. Everything was done to make elevator doors and elevator cars as eye-catching and as attractive as possible.

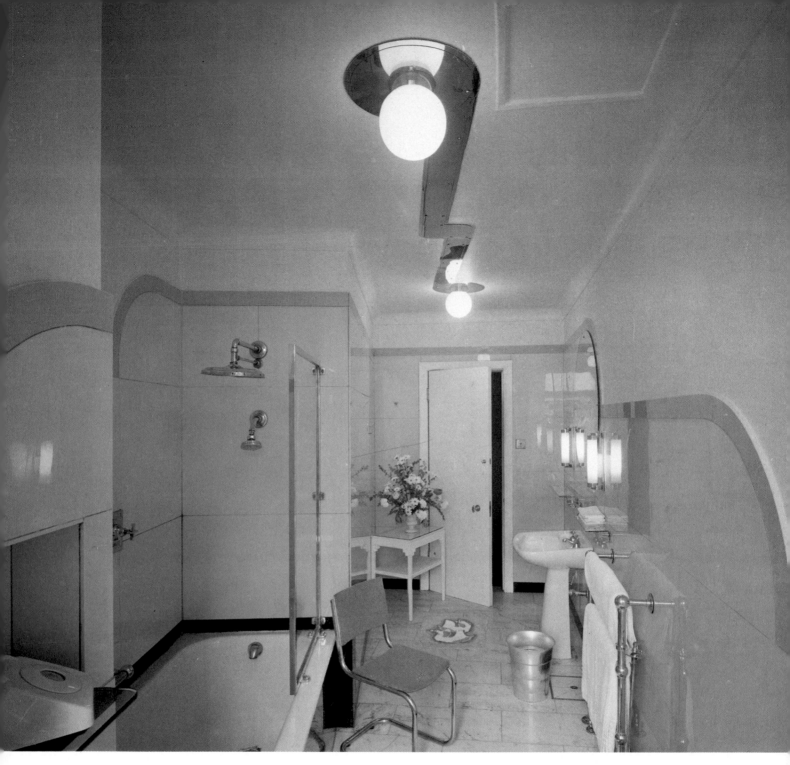

LEFT

Superb wrought-iron mirror by Edgar Brandt. The marble-topped console table is also by Brandt; the two lamps have 'Pâte de verre' shades by Argy-Rousseau. 'Pâte de verre' was a very thick, almost opaque glass; it was used to make vases and ornaments and was particularly effective when used for lampshades, assuming a jewel-like effect when light shone through it. 'Pâte de verre' was a process whereby finished glass was ground into powder, mixed with liquid (usually water) and then cooked in a mould. It was used by a variety of glass designers, notably Argy Rousseau, Décorchemont and Lalique.

ABOVE

A bathroom at Claridge's (c 1930) decorated with the latest glass and chromium fittings; the floor is white speckled marble. It was a comparatively new idea to 'design' a bathroom. Decorators went mad; for instance, Armand-Albert Rateau designed a bathroom for Jeanne Lanvin in which the bath and washbasin were in Siennese yellow marble and the fittings were decorated with butterflies, acanthus leaves, palms and pheasants. But, generally speaking, with improved sanitary fittings, a wide selection of decorative tiles, coloured opaque glass (nitaline) and rubber flooring with jazzy designs, bathrooms could be elegant without too much expense.

FOLLOWING PAGES

The women's lounge on the first mezzanine at Radio City Music Hall, New York. The painted wall decorations are by Yasuo Kuniyoshi, who was born in Japan in 1893, came to America as a young boy and lived and worked there. The 31 smoking-rooms and lounges in Radio City Music Hall are sumptuously decorated and fitted out in various 'modern' styles. Various suitable themes are used: for instance, 'Men Without Women' is the subject of a large abstract mural in the basement men's smoking-room, whilst the women's smoking room on the same floor has a series of murals in white on white parchment depicting 'A History of Cosmetics'.

DECORATIVE OBJECTS

LEFT

A French bronze and ivory figure of a girl dancing and holding a silver ball, signed "Lip". A chryselephantine sculpture (sculpture in ivory and precious metals) was one of the most popular ornaments in a 'modern' drawing room of the 'twenties and 'thirties. Either they were high camp dancing girls in extraordinary poses with amazing hairstyles or headgear; or the more conventional neo-classical figures. The base was usually elegantly shaped in different coloured marbles or in onyx. These figures are now valuable collectors' items and fetch high prices.

RIGHT

Two pieces from the "Wienerwerkstaette" by Hagenauer (c1925); one is a mirror with pewter frame, the other (reflected in the mirror) a free-standing group in polished chrome and ebony. The Vienna workshops were founded in 1903 by Professor Josef Hoffmann, the famous Austrian architect, and this association of artists, designers and craftsmen came to gain great significance. There was hardly a field in which its influence was not felt; interior decorating, furniture, ceramics, enamel, crystal and silver, the graphic arts and fabrics. Gustav Klint, Egon Schiele and Oskar Kokoschka were among the artists who worked for the Werkstaette for a while.

RIGHT

Philips radio with Chinese lacquer work design. Wireless broadcasting was still in its infancy during the 'twenties. When Dame Nellie Melba made her first broadcast in 1920 from Chelmsford she was said to be "the first great operatic celebrity to risk the possible distortion of her voice over the wireless". Radios came in all shapes and sizes, some were outrageously 'modernist', others were designed to tone in with the more conservative backgrounds. The radio illustrated here falls into the second category. Apart from the mere fact of its being a radio, it is the geometric design of the speaker cutting into the decoration that makes it a modern piece of furniture.

British silver partly owes its high standard of workmanship to the interest and patronage of the Worshipful Company of Goldsmiths (where every piece of English silver or silver imported into England goes to be hallmarked). The company encouraged students at art schools and designers in factories to design practical things like tea-sets and cutlery, whilst commissioning artist-craftsmen and small workshops to make exhibition pieces for propaganda purposes at home and abroad. In the illustration the four round boxes are by H G Murphy (all c1930). Of the box with three red balls on top the one-time clerk of the company of goldsmiths writes: "Murphy trying to outdo the Germans in art and decoration and going modern". The little bowl with niello decoration is by Bernard Cuzner (1933), and the cigarette box by C J Shiner.

TOP LEFT
Rectangular pewter tobacco box with stepped lid and formalized flower pattern engraved on sides, designed by A E Poulter (who was a drawing instructor at Kingston Art School) and made by A R Emerson; dating from 1935. Pewter had been very much used by Art Nouveau metalwork designers but seems to have been unfashionable after that period. Although Liberty still advertised artist designed pewter in 'Studio' magazines of the 'twenties and 'thirties, many of the designs dated from around the turn of the century and the later designs are of little interest. It is unusual to find a really successful 'modern' piece like that illustrated here.

TOP RIGHT
Flask and stopper by Maurice Marinot made in 1929. Green glass with black enclosures, acid-etched. Marinot (1882–1960) started life as a painter but gave this up and decided to express his "visions of light and colour" in glass. He was fascinated by strange shapes and textures and was an innovator inasmuch as he introduced bubbles and bulges with planned precision such as the ordinary glass manufacturer would take the greatest pains to eliminate from the finished product. In the 26 years he spent making glass he produced only 2,500 pieces. One of the finest collections of Marinot glass is that given to the Victoria and Albert Museum in 1964 by Florence Marinot.

FAR LEFT
Glass dish on a decorative wrought-iron base, hand-painted on the underside of the glass and signed Quenvit. This artist either painted or enamelled his designs on to glass, using vivid floral patterns with a distinctly geometric feel: it is the decoration rather than the shape of the glass which gives the piece a period style. Following the tradition of earlier French glass designers some of Quenvit's pieces incorporate metalwork. Being hand-painted, his glass is ornamental rather than practical, and was intended for interior decoration first and foremost.

LEFT
Decorative glass vase framed in wrought iron; the glass is by Daum of Nancy, the metal work by Majorelle. Both of these were well known names during the Art Nouveau period as well as the Art Deco period. It is interesting to note the complete change in style that their work underwent. This is particularly noticeable in Majorelle's case. Here his work is angular and geometric. During the Art Nouveau period, however, he designed furniture with the most luxuriant whiplash decorations based on exotic plant motifs. Speckled coloured glass was used by many of the French glass makers at this period, especially Daum and Muller Frères of Luneville.

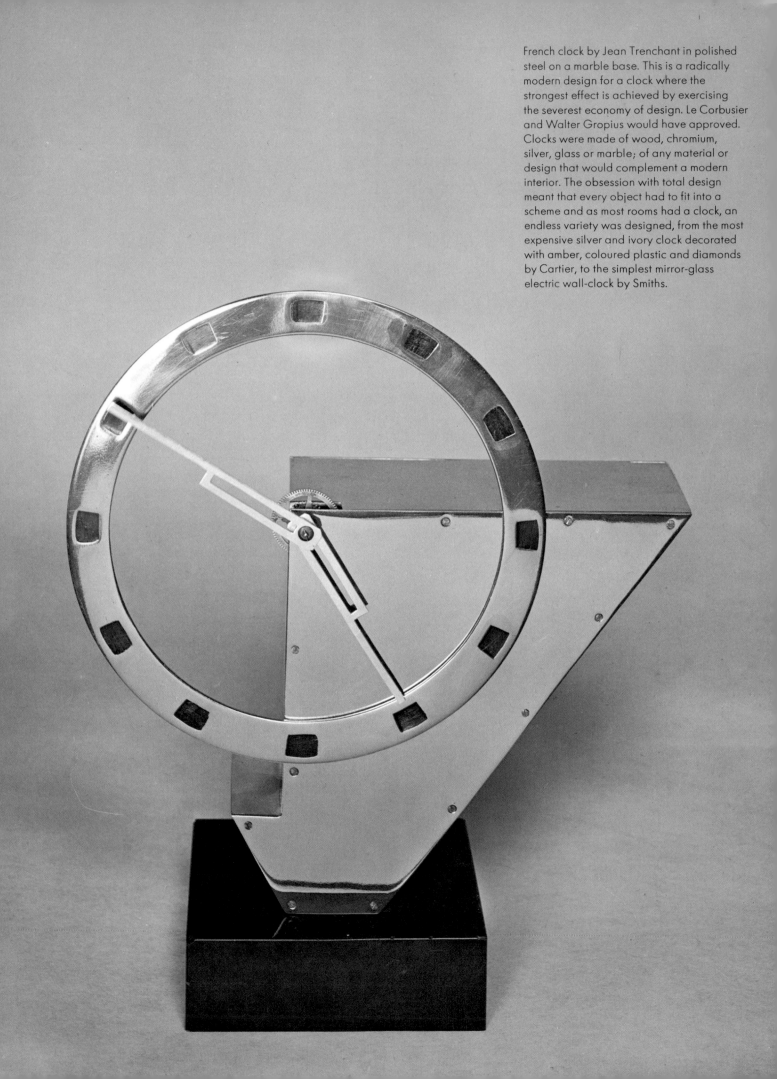

French clock by Jean Trenchant in polished steel on a marble base. This is a radically modern design for a clock where the strongest effect is achieved by exercising the severest economy of design. Le Corbusier and Walter Gropius would have approved. Clocks were made of wood, chromium, silver, glass or marble; of any material or design that would complement a modern interior. The obsession with total design meant that every object had to fit into a scheme and as most rooms had a clock, an endless variety was designed, from the most expensive silver and ivory clock decorated with amber, coloured plastic and diamonds by Cartier, to the simplest mirror-glass electric wall-clock by Smiths.

POTTERY AND PORCELAIN

PREVIOUS PAGE
A collection of porcelain ladies by Doulton, Royal Dux and others. On the top shelf from left to right: the sailor girl is by Royal Dux of Bavaria; Clotilde, the Lido Lady and Columbine by the English firm of Doulton. The bottom shelf contains another Doulton figurine called "Scotties", a pair of sitting ladies (origin unknown) and a pair of amazingly stylized scent bottles (probably German). The green bases contain the perfume and the heads are in fact stoppers to which glass dip-sticks are attached. Figurines of ladies were immensely popular and most of the famous porcelain manufacturers had some in their catalogue.

LEFT
Hand-painted porcelain figure of a dancing pair by Clarice Cliff in her 'Bizarre' series. She is supposed to have designed five different dancing pairs in all. One cannot tell what dance this couple is doing, possibly the tango, which, with the Charleston was all the rage. Tango also lent its name to a burnt orange colour now very much associated with the 'twenties. The ball gown and tails suggest a formal evening occasion rather than an afternoon frittered away at a rango-tea or 'thé dansant'.

BELOW
English bone china coffee set, with silver lustre and pale green design of abstract foliage; produced by A E Gray & Co, Tunstall, Staffs, designed by Susie Cooper and sold by Peter Jones of London. The set is illustrated in the 'Studio Yearbook of Decorative Art' for 1929, where in an article on pottery and glassware it says, "All is not yet well between the artist and the machine, but everything points to the fact that the people are weary of ugliness and will only be satisfied with worthy things worthily made for a worthy purpose." A tremendous effort was made to 'industrialize' the arts and crafts, and as far as ceramics were concerned, to link up the work of the studio potter with industry.

BELOW RIGHT
A group of Belgian ceramic pieces made by Keramis and Boch La Louvière. Most of the pottery by these two firms seems to have a grey-white crackled surface broken by

vividly coloured geometric floral designs in shiny enamelled glazes. Studio pottery was popular in Europe and much space was devoted to ceramics in the 1925 Paris Exhibition. The most interesting (and today valuable) pieces were signed by the artists, and manufacturers encouraged well-known painters to design for them. Bonnard, Derain, Matisse and Vlaminck are among those who designed pottery in France.

RIGHT
Three jazz-musicians made for the Parisian porcelain firm of Robj (c1930). Robj sold decorative figures of all sorts; many of them were useful household objects in disguise. For instance in a set of licqueur bottles, one was a policeman, another a monk; there was a three-piece licqueur set consisting of golfing figures; there was a porcelain lamp in the shape of a cowboy. Most of the figures were slightly comical and cartoon-like. These 'bibelots' were tremendously popular and are now much collected. As the Robj advertisement ran in the 'twenties: 'Les bibelots signés Robj sont le complément de tout intérieur élégant.'

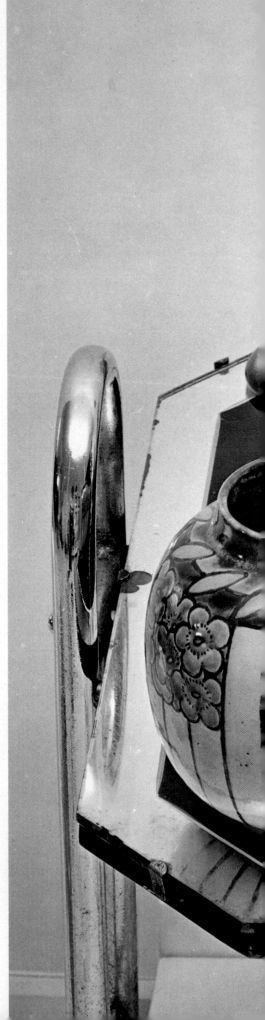

ABOVE
A "Tea for Two" set designed by Clarice Cliff (c1929), one of the most imaginative English designers of tableware of the late 'twenties and 'thirties. Clarice Cliff (1900–1970) first worked at the Burslem firm of A J Wilkinson as an apprentice and was later made Art Director. She produced an astonishing variety of brightly coloured designs, some of them conventional, like her well-known 'crocus pattern', others (in the 'Bizarre' and 'Fantasque' series particularly) more adventurous and abstract. Her table-sets were immensely popular, and were often featured in fashion magazines of the period. Her work was sold in great quantities in Great Britain and was also exported to Australia and New Zealand amongst other countries.

LEFT
A group of plates and vases designed by Charlotte Rhead for Crown Ducal Potteries, probably dating from the mid-'thirties. Charlotte Rhead's work is easily recognizable, with stylized flower and leaf patterns in gay colours, rather reminiscent of floral chintzes, The colours of the designs are painted over an underglazed and contained within the raised outlines of the pattern. This method of obtaining icing-sugar-like outline decoration was known as 'tubeline decoration', and was a very expensive process demanding considerable skill. Most pieces are signed "C Rhead", and a few are signed in full. The plywood trolley on which the pieces are displayed is by Heal's.

A group of salt-glaze ceramic vases decorated by various artists for Royal Doulton (c. 1920–1935). Salt-glaze ceramics had their day in the Victorian era, but Doulton's Lambeth and Burslem potteries continued to produce studio-designed pieces until the Lambeth pottery finally closed in 1957. As with most later Doulton pieces, the vases in this illustration retain basically Victorian shapes, but they are remarkable for their unusual colouring and decoration. Vera Huggins, Eliza Simmance and Bessie Newbury were three of the most distinctive Doulton studio designers of the 'twenties. There was also work by outside artists including Frank Brangwyn and Reco Capey, the Professor of Design at the Royal College of Art.

LEFT
Wall plate by Carter, Stabler, Adams Ltd, Poole Pottery, Dorset; with an impressed mark dating from about 1925. The Poole pottery (still in existence today) was an amalgamation of a tile-making firm and a studio of artists including John Adams, Truda Adams, Harold & Phoebe Stabler and Truda Carter. It is difficult to distinguish between the work of these artists; they all painted in a similar style. But the work of the pottery was very distinctive, usually with decorative stylized birds and flowers hand-painted in delicate pastel colours over a powdered grey glaze. Many pieces by the firm are illustrated in the 'Studio' Decorative Yearbooks.

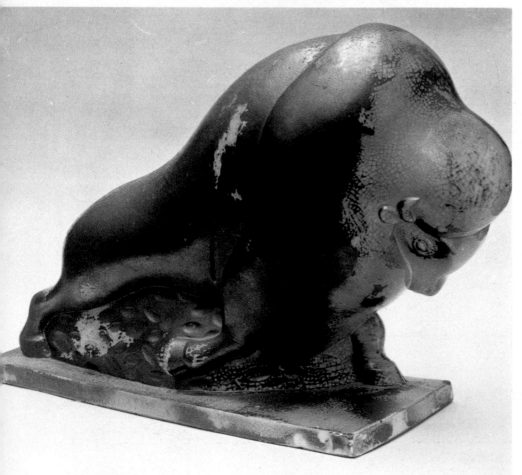

LEFT
Porcelain bison made for Primavera. Primavera was the name of the Art Studio of the Grands Magasins du Printemps in Paris. The studio was established by the Printemps in September 1912 for the creation of decorative art models. In the first year they produced 813 models. An advertisement in the 1928 'Studio' decorative art yearbook goes on to say: "It has developed progressively during the last fifteen years and has now reached the figure of 13,750 models. The creations of the Primavera Studio are produced by its ceramique factory at Sainte Radegonde, near Tours, and by its cabinet works at Montreuil-sous-bois to which are attached workshops for bronzes, sculpture, iron work and decoration in lacquer."

Frontispiece illustration by John Austen to Manon Lescaut, published by Geoffrey Bles in 1928 in an edition limited to 500 copies. John Austen was remarkable for his superb colouring and beautiful line drawing which owes something to the Beardsley tradition. Herbert Grimsditch, in an article in 'Studio' (August 1924), entitled "Mr John Austen and the Art of the Book", says: "Mr Austen makes no claim to illustrate a book in the realistic sense; he does not attempt to represent in line what the word itself should have conveyed to the thoughtful mind, but, taking the book as a book, he decorates it with drawings into which he infuses the spirit of the text".

BELOW
Prometheus, a glazed pottery figure made by Ashtead potteries for Hope's Heating & Lighting Ltd from a design by Percy Metcalfe. It was used by Hope's to advertise the firm. The 'Studio' Yearbook for 1929 says of Ashtead: "The work of the Ashtead Potteries is one of the most remarkable developments of Industrial Art . . . a band of disabled ex-soldiers, broken and worn by years of pain . . . . were set to work with strange tools, upon new and strange fabric. They had no previous training, no apparent predilection for this art or that, but were set down in the potter's studio to learn its technique. Out of a scheme for providing the opportunities to make a livelihood has grown an industry that has already left an indelible mark in matters of sound pottery, good design, real utility, and the satisfying of good taste at small cost."

RIGHT
A random selection of 'twenties and 'thirties song covers. In the 'twenties and particularly the 'thirties with Hollywood musicals in their prime, musical comedy had its heyday. In America tunes by Cole Porter, Jerome Kern, Gershwin, Arlen, Benin, Rogers and Hart filled the air. In England Noel Coward and Ivor Novello enjoyed immense popularity. Amazing Deco sets were built for what is already known as 'the golden age of Hollywood musicals' and Busby Berkeley invented fantastic geometric effects on the screen with his chorus girl routines. Some of all this fantasy was carried over into the colour and design of song covers. There was an enormous market for song albums and sheet music; television had not yet managed to kill live entertainment at home.

BELOW
A vase by Bernardaud & Co of Limoges, made especially for the French furrier 'A La Reine d'Angleterre'. The vase was presumably given away by the firm as an advertisement. Elegant ladies draped in furs float around the vase suspended on clouds. It is not quite clear what furs they are wearing, but the great vogue of the 1920s was for fox, especially for silver fox, though fur of every kind was popular. As real fur was prohibitively expensive substitutes and imitations began to appear. According to James Laver in 'Taste and Fashion' fur was in such great demand that in the late 'twenties there was hardly any fur-bearing animal which was not made to contribute to feminine attire.

PROMETHEUS

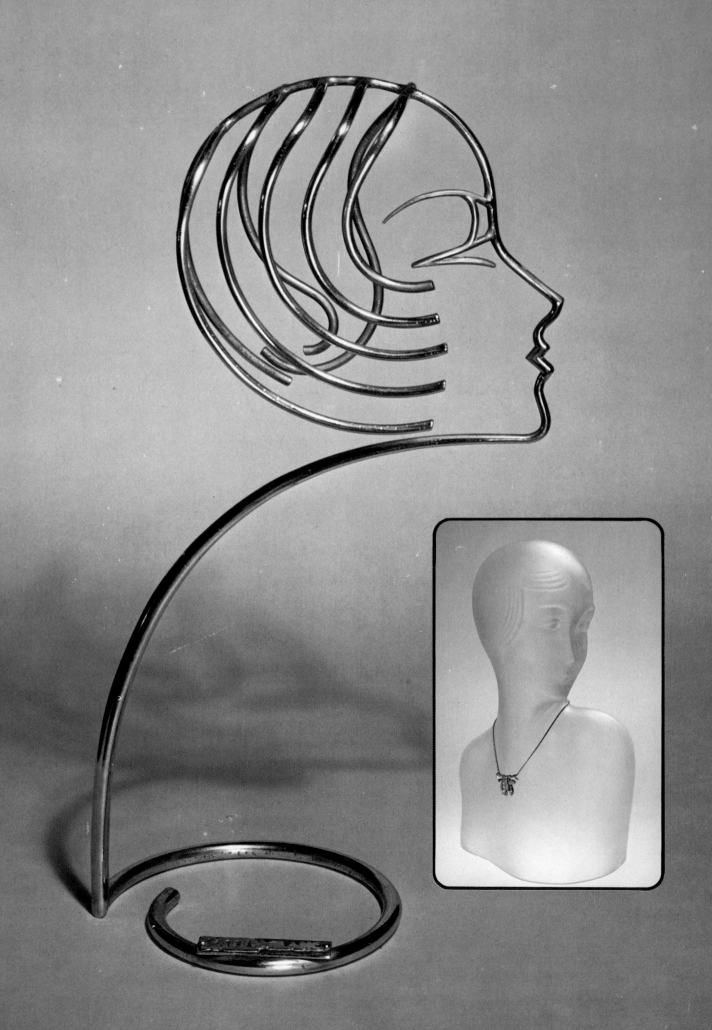

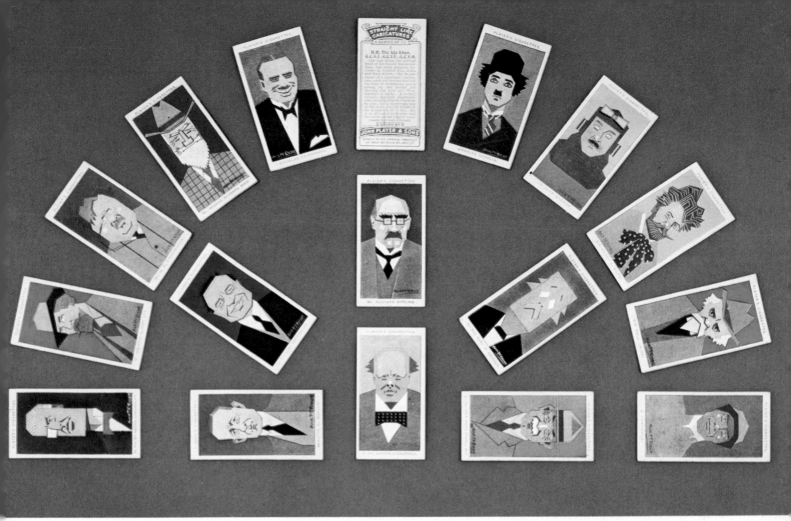

LEFT
Polished chromium hat stand made for the Italian firm of Bazzi in Milan. A supremely simple, supremely elegant design that captures the look and feel of the 'twenties, partly with the use of chromium (which became increasingly popular for all sorts of furniture and fittings), and again with the unmistakably 'twenties boy-girl profile. The shingled hair closely followed the line of the head and made it possible to wear cloche hats which dominated the fashion world from about 1925 to 1930.

Blue ice-glass head, probably used to display hats in a milliner's window: what in the 'twenties was just a shop fitting has today earned itself a place as a minor work of art, and in retrospect looks like a source of pop-art. Ice-glass was used for lamps, lampshades, scent bottles, vases; plates and many other practical and decorative pieces. It came in a great variety of colours and was a cheaper version of the beautiful opalescent glass made famous by Lalique. Marcel waves, as worn by this model, were invented in 1906 by the Parisian hair stylist, Marcel, and became very popular when ladies cropped their hair during the 'twenties, particularly in the late 'twenties when ladies wanted a change from the very severe hairstyles that fashion dictated in the earlier part of the decade.

ABOVE
John Player & Son cigarette cards: a selection from a set of fifty entitled "Straight Line Caricatures" designed by Alick P F Ritchie, and issued in 1926. They are cubist portraits of famous people. Most tobacco firms issued cigarette cards and subjects ranged from 'Pugilists in Action' to 'Our Puppies'. Many sets were devoted to the cinema and film stars. In 'Cigarette Cards and how to collect them' I O Evans says "Most people feel a need, in this mechanical civilization, of some spare-time activity which they can pursue for its own sake. To this end cigarette card collecting has much to recommend it."

RIGHT
Poster designed by E S McKnight Kauffer for Eastman & Son (1922). In the 1924 special poster number of the 'Studio' McKnight Kauffer is described as designing excellent posters "conceived in the modern decorative manner". During the 'twenties posters became bolder and simpler. Their message had to be delivered far more quickly than in Toulouse Lautrec's day. Then the passer-by had time to read and appreciate a poster, but the flapper speeding past at 25 miles per hour had less time to spare. The growing importance of mass-production made publicity vital: a lot of money was spent on poster art

Fabrics . . . that color the lives of women

THE NAME ABERFOYLE on the ends of the board around which the material is rolled assures quality. ABERFOYLE fabrics are fully guaranteed as to quality and fast color. They are dyed in the yarn, then each piece is thoroughly laundered before leaving the mill.

THERE is a fascination for some women in pale pinks and yellows. Through the lives of others may be traced a thread of blue. Color can change a sleeping brunette into a vivacious creature—and color acts like magic on a blonde.

By the shades and tones of their frocks and dresses, women paint their types—just as an artist puts himself into each canvas.

A careful choice between a pale rose voile and a blue and white tissue—the selection of a fabric with a small flowered design rather than a gaily plaided one—then the actual style and making of the frock . . . in these every artist-woman revels.

Among Aberfoyle Fabrics there are materials in many shades and even more designs. In the shops one sees Aberfoyle Fabrics in a palette-ful of shades . . . shades like a color chart from which each woman chooses. The designs are appropriate for every occasion—French designs for summer—bold designs for sport. There's not a colorful piece of Aberfoyle Fabrics but what may be washed as often as you please—washed with soap and water. Aberfoyle Fabrics are on display in shops throughout the country and are distributed to wholesalers by Galey & Lord, Inc., New York City.

Aberfoyle Fabrics

LEFT

Advertisement in the April 1928 issue of 'McCall's', designed by Helen Dryden. 'McCall's' carried some of the most stylish advertisements of the Deco period and back numbers of the magazine reveal some of the the best American graphic design.

It was not only the fashion houses that were design conscious when it came to advertising. Essex cakes, Campbell's soup, Wesson oil or Ipana toothpaste were just a few of the firms whose advertisements seem worth singling out. But in general American poster design before the 'thirties was more traditional than the advertisement for Aberfoyle fabrics illustrated here.

BELOW

A poster advertising Hyde Park, London, designed by Jean Dupas, signed and dated 1930; the caption is a quotation from Samuel Pepys's diaries. This poster was commissioned by the London Underground, and is one of many designed for the railways by famous artists. Martin Battersby refers to Dupas as "a major artist active in the 'twenties". Poster art was treated very seriously between the wars, and a special autumn number of the 'Studio' in 1924 entitled "Posters and their Designers" begins with the words: "This is the day of the poster . . . some of the best brains in the business world of today are concentrated on the possibilities of the poster as a means for advancing trade".

"Thence to Hyde Park, where much good company, and many fine Ladies"

ARCHITECTURE

The BBC building in Portland Place, London, designed by Lt-Col. G Val Mayer with sculptural decorations by Eric Gill and Vernon Hill. It was completed in 1932 and was described in the 'Architectural Review' (August 1932) as parting the road "like a battleship floating towards the observer". The building, referred to as the New Tower of London, excited much criticism for being excessively modern. The 'Architectural Review' said: "The finished building represents the outcome of a struggle between moribund traditionalism and inventive modernism . . . in this case, fortunately, the struggle ended in a victory which largely favoured the modernists."

BELOW

Decorative panels above the main entrance to the 'RCA' Building, Rockefeller Plaza, New York. 'Wisdom' as conceived by the sculptor Lee Lawrie, looks down from the clouds over the central section of the main entrance to the building. Above the flanking sections are figures representing 'light' and 'sound'. The effectiveness of the sculptured treatment is enhanced by the use of polychrome by Leon V Solon, and by the cast glass wall below. The wall, 55 feet long and 15 feet high is moulded in high relief. It is constructed of uniform blocks of glass bonded in vinelite and reinforced by steel rods. The glass was made by the Steuben glass works.

RIGHT

Architectural drawing for a factory in Hammersmith dated 1930. The design is typical of that of many factories built during the early 'thirties: long, low buildings with plenty of glass and an impressive central doorway. Many such buildings are still standing, the most impressive of which is probably the Hoover building at Perivale, just outside London. The buildings and their interior decoration were considered important enough for the 'Architectural Review' to devote considerable space and often whole numbers to factory architecture. As the 'twenties and 'thirties were very design conscious, money spent on designing factories was considered a good investment as they could win prestige and publicity from business clients as well as the general public.

BELOW RIGHT

One of three plaques that decorate the exterior of Radio City Music Hall. The three circular plaques of metal and enamel were designed by Hildreth Meiers and executed by Oscar B Bach. The plaque illustrated here represents the spirit of Drama; the other two represent Song and Dance. The music hall was opened on 27 December 1932; it has a seating capacity of 6,200 and its aim (as the current publicity handout informs us) was "to achieve a complete decorative scheme that is an example of sane modern design, as differentiated from modernistic design that merely takes as a starting point deviation from an established form".

Two views of the Hoover factory on the A40 at Perivale just outside London, built by Wallis, Gilbert & Partners in 1932. Nicholas Pevsner describes it as "perhaps the most offensive of the modernistic atrocities along this road of typical by-pass factories". To the Art Deco enthusiast the effect of streamlining, the brilliant fan-shaped windows going round corners, the linear use of strong colours contrasting with the white of the building, all represent the best in British factory architecture of the period. The decoration above the main entrance of the Hoover building is particularly splendid and has been the subject of much comment. Writers have seen exotic influences of all sorts in the design. Bevis Hillier probably comes closest in his 'World of Art Deco' when he says: "Ballet Russe, Aztec or Egyptian? Even if one could speak to the architect, he might not be able to give an answer." All these influences were present in decorative design at some stage, and designers or architects translated an idea or conglomeration of ideas to fit the modern idiom. Certainly the influence of Le Corbusier and his 'white dream' are felt in factory architecture of the period. "All houses should be white by law" pleaded Le Corbusier; "This cleanliness shows objects in their absolute veracity and implies the obligation of absolute purity." Other factories worth looking at near London are the Firestone Building on the Old London Airport road and the Coty building opposite.

The 1,046 ft Chrysler building is the embodiment of American Deco, particularly the multi-arched dome that tops the structure. The building is faced in Nirosta metal chosen by Walter P Chrysler because it had an "attractive dignified colour similar to platinum". When it was completed in 1930 an article appeared in 'the American Architect' about the designer, William van Alen, who was sometimes known as "the Ziegfield of his profession": it sums up contemporary reaction to the style. "Do you or don't you? That is the question. Some do. Some don't. Some think it's a freak; some think it's a stunt. A few think it is positively ugly; others consider it a great feat, a masterpiece, a 'tour de force'."

ABOVE RIGHT

The Empire State Building, New York, built by Shreve, Lamb and Harmon in 1930. American skyscraper architecture during the 'twenties and 'thirties delighted and surprised the world – it was America's contribution to Art Deco. Many articles have been written about Aztec influences and the pyramid-like shape of skyscrapers. In fact the shape of skyscrapers during the 'twenties and 'thirties was governed principally by the zoning laws of 1916 which produced the set-back arrangement because it was no longer permissible to build towers that rose in a solid mass to enormous heights. The higher a building rose, the narrower the tower had to be in relation to the total ground space occupied by the building, in order to avoid claustrophobic overcrowding and allow in as much light and air as possible at the top of the building.

RIGHT

570 Lexington Avenue, New York; an example of a 1930s modernist skyscraper. This one was built in 1931 by the architects

130

Cross and Cross, whose skyscraper architecture has changed and progressed since then and still continues to enhance the New York skyline. Arnold Lehmann, in 'The Metropolitan Museum of Art Bulletin' (April 1971), writes of skyscrapers of the period as "proudly individualistic towers of the nineteen-twenties and thirties, those 'cathedrals of commerce' and castles in the sky". This particular building was the headquarters of 'RCA' until that company moved to Rockefeller Center. The terracotta crown of the brick-tower was meant to symbolize "the radio waves and electric power of RCA".

COCKTAILS AND LAUGHTER

L'ECHO DE PARIS

Evening frocks from 'McCall's', April and July 1928. This American magazine featured the latest dress designs from Paris every month. A fashion editor's note tells you that smartly gowned young women filled the bustles on their evening gowns with tissue paper the colour of the fabric. "You know the trick by the crackle of the paper as they sit down." Paper patterns for all dresses illustrated in 'McCall's' were available at an average price of 45 cents. These patterns came in during the early 'twenties and were dictated by the rapidly diminishing clientele able to afford couturier's prices, and the ever-growing demand for fashionable but inexpensive clothes.

RIGHT

A standing cabinet inlaid with veneers in at least ten different kinds of wood, perhaps Portuguese. The stars are mother of pearl and the decoration round the coach lamp is inlaid brass. The scene depicts a lady in fancy dress standing in front of her carriage and obviously on the way to or from a 'bal masqué'. Fancy dress became very popular just after World War I; the Paris fashion designer Paul Poiret threw extravagant fancy-dress parties that were ruinously expensive. At least they helped to make his salon the most exclusive in Paris and set society on its path through the "roaring twenties".

RIGHT

Silver-plated modernist cocktail set with six cocktail goblets and a shaker; from the Paris workshop of Donald Desny. Classical Deco shapes are used here in designing containers for that classical Deco addiction, the cocktail. Here the novelty lies not in a joke idea but in streamlined modernism. The French designers produced some of the most elegant sets; for instance those that came from the Baccarat workshops with severe geometric patterns in black and white glass. Desny worked mostly in metal. There is a pure silver version of this set which sometimes comes with a matching glass and metal tray.

ABOVE
Cocktail cabinet by Maples of London dating from the 'thirties, with original decanters, glasses, cocktail shaker and lemon squeezer. This beautifully designed piece of furniture is in veneered maple wood with chrome fittings and blue mirror glass. The cocktail cabinet was a comparitively new piece of furniture, the mark of a changing society. Servants were no longer available to prepare elaborate dinner parties and the easiest way of entertaining was to invite people to cocktails. Most cocktail cabinets were designed to fit in with modernist interiors, but if a cabinet was required to fit into a room with antique furniture something suitable like an antique sideboard might be discreetly converted to conceal cocktail gear.

TOP RIGHT
A page from the 'Savoy Cocktail Book' complied by Harry Craddock, the barman at the Savoy Hotel, London. The book was published in 1930 with charming colour illustrations and decorations by Gilbert Rumbold. It contains everything the cocktail addict might need to know like the information that cocktails were named after "Coctel", the beautiful daughter of King Axolotl VIII of Mexico. It has recipes for

anything from a 'Bosom Caresser' to an 'Alabama Fizz' and it has a section entitled "a few hints for young mixers" – hint no. 4 is "shake the shaker as hard as you can: don't just rock it; you are trying to wake it up, not send it to sleep." The cocktail glasses and sticks date from the same period.

FAR RIGHT
Yellow glass cocktail shaker with hand-painted sunburst and cockerel decorations, and silver stopper and strainer combined with 1936 hallmark. The sunburst was perhaps the favourite English decorative device of the 'thirties; one associates it particularly with the glass in front doors of suburban homes or with enamelled compacts and cigarette cases, but it was very common in furniture and interior design of all sorts. There is a charming book called 'The English Sunrise' by Brian Rice and Tony Evans with a series of seventy-six photographs showing the sunrise as a decorative symbol. Most of the illustrations show designs dating from the 'twenties and 'thirties.

TOP FAR RIGHT
"The navy-blue ghost of Mr Blaker, the allegro negro cocktail-shaker": a quotation from 'Façade' by Edith Sitwell. The Negro cocktail shaker is used here as the design

for a combined table-lighter and cigarette dispenser by Ronson. The barman shakes away at a 'Fizz' behind his up-to-the-minute bar with its chrome streamlining and cocktail paraphernalia. The central section of the bar conceals a Ronson touch-tip lighter, and on each side the bar tops flip up to reveal a spring-loaded cigarette container. There was a whole series of these joke lighters. Another was designed so that, after pressing a lever, a slightly cubist monkey bent over to pick up a cigarette which had rolled out of a chrome and enamel dispenser.

RIGHT
English silver and enamel ladies' cigarette case (hallmarked 1931), with two dancing figures in brightly coloured costumes against a black background. On the back of the case there is a cherub in pink enamel on a blue background. The costumes are undoubtedly inspired by the work of Léon Bakst whose designs for ballets like 'Scheherezade' brought a middle Eastern look to Paris fashion for a while. Paul Poiret, whilst freeing women from their corsets, imprisoned them in hobble skirts. Although the baggy pantaloons on the cigarette case are reminiscent of the Kazbah, the zig-zags, cubes and geometric flowers, are pure European Art Deco.

ACKNOWLEDGEMENTS

Publisher and authors would like to express their grateful thanks to the following individuals and organizations for their help in providing colour transparencies or items for special photography.

Mrs. & Mrs. Peter Alexander 80 right; Michael Andrews, 13 below, 21 above left, 38 above, 50, 51 above and centre; Richard & Rodney Bennet 79, 87; Bethnal Green Museum London 8, 34 above right, below left & below right, 36 above right & below right, 37, 41, 42, 43, 45 above & below, 48 below right, 58 below right, 71; Brighton Museum 93 above & below, 94 above left & below right, 98 below, 103 above, 118 below; Butler & Wilson 83, 85 below, 91 below; Calouste Gulbenkian Foundation 17, 20 below, 56, 57 below; Barrie Chilton 115 below; Editions Graphiques Gallery, London 7, 18 above & below, 22 left, 39, 40 above, 46, 47 above & below, 48 left, 49, 51 below, 60, 64 above 65, 66 above & below, 88, 91 above; Geffrye Museum, Shoreditch, London 11, 34 above left, 52 right; Keith Gibson 28 below; Goldsmiths & Silversmiths Company Limited 110 above left, 111; The Hamlyn Publishing Group 28 above, 29 above, 30 below, 31, 35 below; Mr. Nelson Hargreaves 14; Averil Hart 110 below right; Haworth Art Gallery, Accrington, 21 above right; High Camp, London 72, 124 below; Bevis Hillier 134; Michael Holford Photographs 10; John Jesse 81, 112, 122, 124 above; Karl-Ernst-Osthaus-Museum, Hagen, Germany 62 below; Dan Klein 80 below, 82 above & below, 86, 89 above, 108, 109 above & below, 110 below left, 113, 116 below, 118 above, 122 inset, 123 above, 135 above left, above right & below left; Klingspor Museum, Otterlo, Holland, 21 below; Knoller-Muller Stichting 61 below; John Lyons 120 left; Mansell Collection, London, 15; Martins Forrest Collection 84 above, 92, 95, 96 right, 119, 135 below right; William Morris Gallery, Walthamstow, London, 6, 9, 61 above, 62 above; Munchener Stadsmuseum, 13 above; Munch-Musset, Oslo, 64 below; Museum of Modern Art, New York, 33 above; Lillian Nassau Gallery, New York, 32, 44 centre and below, 59; Diana & Simon Nicholson 78, 114 above; L'Odeon, London; 90, 115 above; Mr. Van Phillips 23, 24 above & below, 25, 26 above, 35 above; Nigel Quiney 103 below, 116-117; Michael Raeburn 85 above, 114 below; Rapho Agence de Presse, 26 below left, 27 above; Sunday Times Syndication, 2, 16, 36 left, 54 below, 63; Sybarites Gallery New York, 94 above right, 96 left, 104 above, 133 above; Victoria & Albert Museum, Crown Copyright, 53 above, 58 above left & right, 68-69, 71, 89 below, 110 above right, 133 below, back ends; Geoffrey Warren ends, 22 below right, 33 below left, 53 below, 54 above, 55, 67, 88 below; Peter Wentworth Shields 116 above, 123 below, 127 above; M.J.P. Ziolo, 12, 26 below right, 27 below, 30 above, 57 above;

Photography by:—

Michael Dyer Associates: ends, title page left, 4, 6, 7, 8, 9, 11, 13 below, 18 above & below, 19, 20 above, 21 above left, 22 left & above right, 33 below left & below right, 34, 36 above right & below right, 37, 38 above & below, 39, 40 above & below, 41, 42, 43, 44 above, 45 above & below, 46, 47 above & below, 48 left, above right & below right, 49, 50, 51 above, centre and below, 52 left & right, 53 below, 54 above, 55, 58 below right, 60, 61 above, 62 above, 64 above, 65, 66 above & below, 67.

Angelo Hornak: title page right, 3, 68-136

30 ROCKEFELLER PLAZA

SUNKISSED

SUNWEAR AND THE HOLLYWOOD BEAUTY 1930-1950

This publicity photo for *Second Fiddle* shows a great variety of swimsuits for 1939.

Book Design *Wade Daughtry, Collectors Press, Inc.*
Editor *Lisa Perry*

We are always seeking to expand our collection.
If you are interested in selling your pin-up originals
or ephemera please contact Collectors Press, Inc.

For a free catalog write to:

COLLECTORS PRESS, INC.

P.O. Box 230986
Portland, OR 97281
Toll Free 1 800 423 1848
collectorspress.com

Printed in Singapore

9 8 7 6 5 4 3 2 1

Library of Congress Cataloging-in-Publication Data
Curtis, Joshua.
Sunkissed : swimwear and the Hollywood beauty / by Joshua
Curtis ; foreword by Ann Rutherford.
        p. cm.
ISBN 1-888054-77-8 (hardcover w/jacket)
1.   Glamour photography. 2. Celebrities-California-
Los Angeles-Portraits. 3.Bathing suits-History--20th century. I.
Title.
TR678 .C87 2003
779'.24--dc21
2002015205

Sunkissed

SUNWEAR AND THE HOLLYWOOD BEAUTY 1930-1950

JOSHUA JAMES CURTIS

COLLECTORS PRESS

PORTLAND, OREGON

LUPE VELEZ
1908- 1944

NORMA JEANE DOUGHERTY
1926- 1962

CAROLE LANDIS
1919- 1948

Dedication

This work is dedicated to these six extraordinary women.

Each touched so many lives and yet unhappy with their own.

The joy they bring to millions will forever outweigh their

sorrow in life and love.

MARIE McDONALD
1923- 1965

BARBARA BATES
1925- 1969

DOROTHY DANDRIDGE
1923- 1965

Contents

Acknowledgments

Norma Jean Dougherty, 1945.
Norma Jean is a model for the Blue
Book Modeling Agency at the time of
this photograph, she will soon become
Marilyn Monroe. Suit by Catalina.

There are many people I would like to thank for making this work a reality. First of all, Ralph Bowman, who unselfishly opened his remarkable pin-up collection to me. Couldn't have done it without you. Michael Ripley, who helped in so many aspects of this project, including acting as chauffeur. Thanks for putting up with me, buddy. Al Morley for also putting up with me. Patrick Picking and his wonderful website. Michael Fitzgerald for his vast knowledge of Hollywood and the people in it. Beth at Mailboxes, Etc., for her tireless efforts during my quest. My best pal, Colonel Gerald G. Robinson, for his support. He is one of the best squadron commanders that World War II ever saw. My loving parents and brothers; thanks for all the computer knowledge, Mikie. Meghan Ivey, whose voice keeps the thirties and forties eras alive; thanks for not letting me go. Dorothy Morris and Caren Marsh for always being there for me; I'll love you always. Ginger Rogers, who could not see this final product but inspired me early on to "get that book done." Ann Rutherford, sweetheart, your support and love is inspiring to me. Gloria DeHaven whose friendship and love is a treasure to me. Barbara Hale, dear, you don't know how much you helped on this project. When things were looking bleak, you were there for me. Marsha Hunt and Lynne Brighton, whose belief in me is much appreciated. Georgia Lee, I love you. The late George Montgomery, a fine actor and artist, who always inspired me with, "keep it up, you'll go a long way." Joy Hodges for all your faith and belief in my talents; thanks for all you've done through the years. Coleen Gray, you're a joy. Joan Leslie, a wonderful talent. Thanks for all your time. Gloria Jean, Carole Mathews, and Jean Porter: thanks for the time you spent with me. For sharing their private collections with me, my gratitude goes to Shirley Buchanan, Barbara Hale, Sybil Jason, Gloria Jean, Caren Marsh, Trudy Marshall, Carole Mathews, Dorothy Morris, Jean Porter, Ann Rutherford, Penny Singleton, and Esther Williams. Lest we forget: Murray Juveiler, Frob, Gerri Brooks, Paul O'Brien, Aaron Rosenburg, The Gang at A&E, Debra Mitchell, Paul Umbriago, Amber Soest, Margo Essman, Peter Perez, the staff of the Yucaipa Library, Sarah Lissy, Robert Aragon, Mike Constable, Jim Heimann, Vince Brown, Sabin Gray, Brittany, Debbie, and Bert. To all the fine photographers whose work is represented here: Bert Anderson, Ernest A. Bachrach, Russell Ball, Clarence Bull, Eric Carpenter, Robert Coburn, Schuyler Crail, Don English, Ed Estabrook, Tom Evans, Roman Fruelich, Durward Graybill, Fred Hendrickson, George Hurrell, Ray Jones, Alex Kahle, Gene Kornman, Irving Lippman, Hal McAlpin, Floyd McCarty, John Miehle,

"Morgan," Thalmage Morrison, Frank Powolny, Charles Rhodes, Eugene Robert Richee, A.L. "Whitey" Schafer, Ned Scott, Bert Six, Sprague Talbott, Joe Walters, and Scotty Welbourne. Apologies to those unknown photographers whose work may appear herein. To the studios that made it all happen: Columbia, Hal Roach, Metro Goldwyn Mayer, Paramount, Republic, RKO, Twentieth Century Fox, Universal, and Warner Bros.

FOREWARD

Ann Rutherford, 1940.

People come in all shapes and sizes, and there's a bathing suit for every shape and every size. If we didn't have bathing suits, we wouldn't have that mad rush in the spring to take a little weight off before shopping for a new suit. There's nothing wrong with showing yourself off in a bathing suit. Look back to the turn of the century and think of the choices women had in bathing suits. The usual "costume" consisted of a knee-length wool dress, gloves, hat, black wool stockings, and pumps laced to the knee. It's a marvel that they didn't all drown! Wool gets very heavy when it's wet, but it seemed to have been the only material available in the early 1900s. When I was a child living in San Francisco, we went to an incredible swimming place called the Sutro baths* with nine plunges, as they called them, fountains, and everything. We didn't have our own bathing suits, so we rented them. The attendants would size you up as you walked in, and for little kids, they usually handed you a suit that was a pretty good fit. I can still remember them being itchy and scratchy. It was a big breakthrough in the thirties when they made those lovely satin Lastex suits. The one-piece version was my favorite. Playsuits-I just loved them. I lived in them. They were so comfortable, and I could wear them anywhere because people weren't "stuffy" in those days. When you were young, they took advantage of youth and a bathing suit. There was nothing wrong with that. We had to model a great deal of sunwear for many "holiday art" publicity shots: like jumping over three-foot long firecracker props for Independence Day. The publicity people were very imaginative, trying to use a bathing suit for every holiday, from Christmas on down. On the morning of the photo photos, the studio would send over a limousine to pick me up at my house. In the car would be the driver, a photographer, and a publicity woman. It was the publicist's job to round up the bathing suits in the proper size and have them waiting in the backseat of the car. The limousines all had little silk roller blinds that you could pull down. On the way to the beach, I could change my clothes right in the car and arrive ready to jump out. Sometimes, if I had to make several changes, and we were shooting near somebody's house, the people would come out to watch. We would chat and get friendly, and they would invite us in. Sometimes I would end up changing in their home. During the day, we'd break and go some place at the beach for a leisurely lunch, come back, change again, and take more pictures. I remember bringing back bread from a restaurant, a few slices that were left at the table, and feeding the birds. But to really get the message out to the birds, I eventually took a whole loaf of bread. I started picking it apart into big crumbs and chumming it. Then the birds squeaked and squawked and came right out of the blue. I had enough of it to throw great handfuls in the air at once, and the photographer was there ready with his camera. That was a very special photograph. This kind of shoot was publicity for the bathing suit manufacturer or the store that loaned the suits. I seldom recall getting them wet, but when I did, they usually had to give them to me. What a pity! Occasionally, the manufacturer asked if I had a favorite suit. In that case, it would be given to me. This book is for all generations to leaf through and see *The Way We Wore*,** to quote the title of Marsha Hunt's book. *Sunkissed* has universal appeal and is a good accompaniment to Turner Classic Movies or American Movie Classics. It's amazing how some of these fashions still can be worn today. And it's interesting to see what people looked like when they were girls, yes, or when they were boys.-*Ann Rutherford 2001*

*This massive glass palace contained one fresh water tank, five saltwater tanks at various temperatures, and a large saltwater tank at ocean temperature. Crowds numbering up to 1,600 could play on slides, trapezes, springboards, and a high dive. All in all, the Baths offered for rent 20,000 bathing suits and 40,000 towels.** Hunt. The Way We Wore: Styles of the 1930s and '40s and Our World Since Then. Fallbrook, California: Aero Publishers, Inc., 1993.*

INTRODUCTION

A hh, yes. Sunkissed. The lovely girls of yesteryear donning some of Hollywood's smartest sunwear fashions with their perfectly soft skin kissed by the rays of the sun. Hollywood of yesteryear would make you believe everything was copasetic and what with the Depression and World War II, maybe this facade was greatly needed. Certainly men and women alike who devoured magazines welcomed pin-ups featuring their Hollywood favorites. In reality, some actresses featured in this book weren't allowed by their studios to get a tan. Actresses Dorothy Morris and Caren Marsh remember the stress put upon them to stay fair-skinned for the movie cameras. What the actresses did have in common was being able to model some of the most delectable fashions of the twentieth century. Though most high fashion came in the form of evening wear, some wonderfully creative designs were found to be suited for the sun. Along with a wonderful smile, these girls can be quite irresistible. But don't let that smile fool you. The smile comes with the photograph. It does not necessarily reflect the feelings the actress might have had at that moment. Some of these girls were unhappy in life. Some took their own lives, and it is they to whom this book is dedicated. Some like Bette Davis and Olivia de Havilland had long battles with their studios to earn the respect they deserved. Still, some of these girls were having the time of their lives and loving every minute of it, and their smiles reflect this. Actresses such as Marsha Hunt and Ann Richards refused to do "leg art" fearing it would interfere with their hard-won stature of a serious actress. Still other actresses such as Greer Garson were deemed to be "above" leg art. Big stars such as Joan Crawford, Bette Davis, Jane Wyman, and Ginger Rogers continued to model sunwear long after receiving Academy Awards. For many actresses, the award was indeed the end to such publicity. On the other hand, Betty Grable and Esther Williams could hardly be imagined without a bathing suit. Their studios not only cultivated these images but made millions of dollars doing so. Ida Lupino displayed her petite form for many a year before directing and screenwriting – fields long dominated by men in Hollywood. Ann Sheridan expressed her desire for shedding her "Oomph Girl" status in 1942. "Pinning the label of 'Oomph Girl' on me was the thing that almost created a monster in my life. Perhaps I never would have rated any special notice if this freak publicity stunt hadn't received such unexpected attention. On the other hand, my reputation as the 'Oomph Girl' far surpassed my latent ability as an actress." Peggy Moran, daughter of famous pin-up artist Earl Moran, just may have been the real "Peggy, the Pin-up Girl." Contrary to popular belief, Peggy did not model for her father, but she did have admirers on "both sides of the fence" during World War II. "Some of the soldiers in the Pacific," she recalls, "sent me a photo of myself and wrote, 'We found this on a dead Japanese.' It came from a magazine or newspaper he had folded in his knapsack. "This clipping, no doubt, was removed from a dead American soldier by the Japanese soldier who met the same fate. "I didn't want him to come gunning and looking for me!" she adds. Jane Russell was a phenomenon in her own right. She attained great fame and a flurry of fans without ever being seen in films. She made *The Outlaw* in 1941, but because of controversy surrounding the film's sexual overtones, the film was released for only a short period in 1943 and not officially released until 1950. Everyone wanted to know who this sexual dynamo was that was being kept off the movie screens. The publicity stills sure kept the people from guessing, though. Child actress Gloria Jean recalls when she became aware of growing up, "I came to the sudden realization, when they started putting swimsuits and things like that on me, that I was getting older and getting out of those child parts. It was okay, but I never considered myself that type." Regardless, save for a handful of actresses, "leg art" publicity in various sunwear creations was taken of each actress who signed up with a major studio. It wasn't questioned. It was expected. In some cases it marked the initial entrance by a new young talent to the public relations world of Hollywood. Still, many girls enjoyed this form of publicity and were very proud of themselves physically. For instance, Ina Ray Hutton, who led her own "All Girl Orchestra," even made a one-reeler film that featured her leading her band in nothing but a bathing suit. Men did their share of sunwear publicity as well, not to the degree that women did, but how creative can a designer get with a pair of shorts anyway? Clark Gable, Errol Flynn, Joel McCrea, John Payne, and Robert Preston were just few of the actors seen poolside, fishing, or surfing the ocean blue. You could readily find these photos on the hallowed confines of many a co-ed's walls or stored safely in their history books. The studio publicity departments made sure their stars, or starlets, appeared as perfect as can be. This came in the form of photo "touch ups." Wrinkles were smoothed out or eliminated, and freckles vanished with studio artists' special touches to the photographs. Studios called on cosmetic surgeons as well if an actress had any permanent imperfections. "Little slight adjustments were made as they went along: a little bit here, a little bit there, a tuck here, and a tuck there," relates Ann Rutherford. "But it was never spoken of anymore than anybody mentioned the fact that Franklin D. Roosevelt was confined to a wheelchair." Although not kind to all, Hollywood was a playground for many. Its citizens found life and work in the town to be rewarding and adventurous. Gloria De Haven lovingly declares, "I adored doing all that stuff. It was never a chore for me. It was a wondrous experience." Ann Rutherford likens her experience in Hollywood to "stealing money without a gun." The thirties and forties proved an exciting time for sunwear as well. This is especially true with swimwear. Manufacturers competed to introduce more aerodynamic and comfortable suits using more diverse materials and fabrics. The emphasis of change was placed on the cut of the bathing suit, allowing for more tanning. In 1931, Jantzen introduced "The Shouldaire" for such a purpose. The Jantzen catalog described the suit as having a "necklace Shouldaire cord . . . when tied about the neck (it) permits the dropping of the shoulder straps for an even coat of tan all over the entire back and shoulders. This feature minimizes the possibility of shoulder strap marks that are sometimes apparent when low-cut evening gowns are worn." Ginger Rogers, described as a featured player for Warner Bros., was the model. The move from 100 percent wool suits to cotton, linen, sharkskin, rayon, and satin Lastex was a welcome change as well. Rayon was the first manufactured fiber. It made its appearance in France in the 1890s as "artificial silk,"and the name Rayon was adopted in 1924. Dr. Wallace H. Carothers created nylon for Du Pont in the 1930s. First called Nylon 66, this material found its way into playsuits along with rayon and cotton. It took a tire company to introduce what was at the time the best material for swimsuits. In the 1930s Dunlop invented a combination of latex rubber and ammonia that their researchers called Lastex. It was an elastic yarn that was woven into various materials to give elasticity. Lastex and silk Lastex became popular swimsuit materials. Some of the manufacturers Hollywood liked to promote were Catalina, Cole of California, Jantzen, and Mabs of Hollywood. (This certainly was with the encouragement of the manufacturer.) In 1947 Catalina's head designer, Mary Ann DeWeese, teamed with Hollywood's top studio designers to introduce new designs for that year. The list included Travis Banton, Milo Anderson, Edith Head, Howard Shoup, Vera West, Renie, and Edward Stevenson. In any case, these companies and many more were in constant competition to please the public and their shareholders. Commenting on this era, one actress states, "The manufacturers followed each other so closely and knocked each other off with such shame. The minute something was out, it was smuggled out of the plant and somebody would copy it on the way home. I mean they had spies every place. If you were in the manufacturing business, you had to have loyal employees. Otherwise, if they could draw at all, they would draw somebody else a bathing suit for a fee." Actors and actresses alike modeled these creations for their studios' publicity and the manufacturers' advertisements and catalogs. Playsuits were the rage during the "golden age of Hollywood." More comfortable than bathing suits, these primarily one-piece creations could be worn shopping or to the market – especially the open-air markets in California. These suits were made of light fabrics like cotton, linen, nylon, rayon, and sometimes gabardine. The same materials were implemented in the many wonderful shorts and halter creations of the time. These two-piece designs highlighted the wearer's bare midsection. Not only did midriff outfits appear in sunwear, but the fad crept into eveningwear as well. The bellybutton was rarely seen in public, however, in any of these creations till about 1948. At least, not in the United States. The biggest advent in swimwear actually came from France in 1946 in the form of the "bikini." This set the tone for brevity in swimwear for years to come. Today's creations all trace their heritage to the glorious fashions illustrated in this volume.

The Thirties

Karen Morley, in a wool two-piece at Palos Verdes, had more than 30 films to her credit when this photo was taken in 1936. You may remember her from the original *Scarface* in 1932.

"It's kinda fun, you look back and think—
I didn't wear that, and did I do that."
-GLORIA JEAN

"Nobody was ever that young!"
-ANN RUTHERFORD

"I thought Paulette Goddard
was beautiful."
-GLORIA DeHAVEN

"You could put two fingers
around my waist."
-JOY HODGES

"When I was six a fortune
teller put his hand under my
chin and said 'Oh an actress'
and walked on. I believed it."
-PEGGY MORAN

Una Merkel was Lillian Gish's stand-in before appearing herself in films in 1923. The shoes are made of rubber.

Yes, that's **Myrna Loy** between **Doris Hill** and **Jane Winton** wearing typical swimwear of the late 1920s. The characters have been sewn on these 100 percent wool suits as a personal touch. Myrna devoted most of her time to the Red Cross during World War II. Photograph, 1926.

Helen Kane, the "boop-boop-a-doop" girl introduced her charming rendition of "I Wanna Be Loved By You" in 1928 which resulted in her motion picture contract, just in time for the talkies. 1930 saw her last film. This cute number has a matching cape, scarf, and parasol.

Red-haired **Clara Bow** was such a sensation in the 1920s that she was labeled the "It Girl." Of course she appeared in a movie called *it*, but audiences soon learned she had "it" as well. Clara wears rubber shoes with her wool swimsuit in this 1928 image.

Wynne Gibson began her film career in 1929 after having been a chorus girl since 15 years of age. She usually portrayed gangsters' molls and tramps in her films. 1987 saw her passing after living with her girlfriend for many years. In these photographs, from her personal collection, Wynne models a Catalina "Bandeau suit" in red and white from 1933.

"You know, my film career began in 1929!", A very proud **Ginger Rogers** exclaimed to the author in 1995. Yes, 1929 was the beginning of a love affair between motion pictures and lovely Ginger. Her first feature film was released a year later. Personally, she delighted guests at home with her own soda fountain rather than a bar.

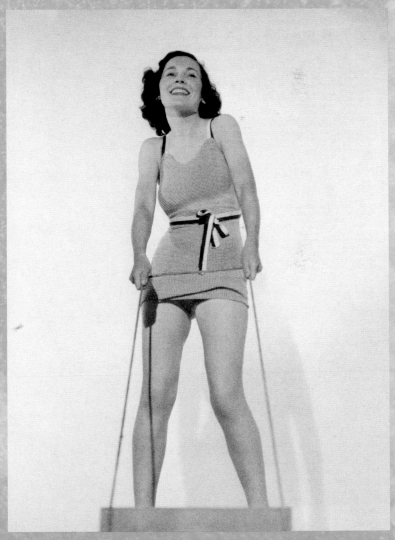

Maureen O'Sullivan is best remembered as "Jane" from the old *Tarzan* movie series.

Lupe Velez publicizes Hal Roach studios, 1935.

Joan Crawford.

Ann Sheridan models a cotton broadcloth playsuit in navy and white, 1935.

Dolores Del Rio enjoyed movie success in Hollywood and her homeland of Mexico, as well. Born in Durango, she began her film career in 1925 in the US and continued making films in Mexico from 1943 on.

Volleyball on Malibu Beach with **Ruth Rogers** and **Marion Weldon,** 1938.

Ann Rutherford in a wool two-piece for a Newport, California, photo shoot, 1938.

Young starlet, **June Lang** (left), was a dancer known as June Vlasek when she began films in 1931. She would be known as Lang three years later.

Dixie Lee Crosby shows off the wonders of cellophane, introduced in the 1920s, in this provocative photo. Can you get more casual than this? Bing Crosby and Dixie Lee were married from 1930 to 1952.

Jean Arthur appeared on screen from 1923 till 1953 and gave many wonderful comedic performances. She was one of Frank Capra's favorite actresses and had her own television show in the 1960s.

Olivia de Haviland and **Anita Louise,** 1937.

Katharine Hepburn.

Maxine Reiner in polka dot suit of rich deep blue, and **Dolores Casey** in a suit of pale green and white stripes, 1935.

Lyda Roberti's bold print sarong features matching sandals,1934. From Warsaw, Poland, Lyda's unique singing style was enjoyed by many till her untimely death of a heart attack in 1938 at the age of 31. Inspired by the Tahitian natives, this suit was called the "Pareo Tahitian."

Anita Page.

Carole Lombard in an elegant black silk pajama.

Mary Carlisle appeared in numerous films between 1930 and 1943.

Betty Gillette appeared in several movies in the early
1930s and then again in the mid-1940s, mostly uncredited.
Her wool knit suit is complemented with hat of straw.

A young **Bette Davis** with a playsuit of corduroy.

Claire Trevor enjoys the sands of Malibu in this maroon and white suit of wool knit.

Philadelphian **Elizabeth Russell** in one of her early publicity shots, models a daring cotton three-piece, 1936. She would go on to make more than 20 films.

Anita Page wears a suit made of bandannas tied together.

Benny Goodman and **Martha Raye** swing it for *The Big Broadcast* of 1937, 1936. The playsuit is perfect for Lindy Hopping.

Maxine Jennings, two-piece features shorts with zipper pocket, 1936.

Claire Trevor sports her personal box pleated red and white print playsuit designed by Fox studio stylist William Lambert, 1936.

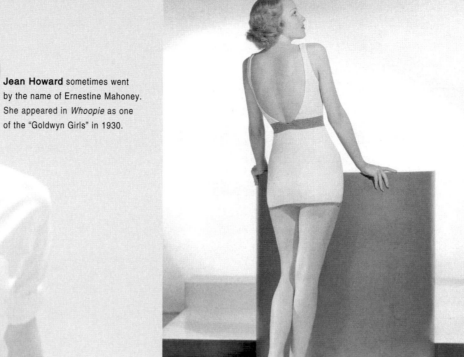

Jean Howard sometimes went by the name of Ernestine Mahoney. She appeared in *Whoopie* as one of the "Goldwyn Girls" in 1930.

Frances Farmer was such a fascinating subject to Nirvana's Kurt Cobain that she inspired the song "Frances Farmer will have her revenge on Seattle." Our little inspiration is photographed here in 1937 at the start of her rocky and controversial career.

Janet Gaynor strolls the beach near Venice. Janet was the first actress to receive a Best Actress Academy Award in 1928.

Olympe Bradna was a performer with the Follies Bergere in France before coming to Hollywood. She is 17 years old here, 1937.

Forever remembered as King Kong's first gal pal in 1933, beautiful Fay Wray actually began films 14 years previous when just 13 years old. She models a red and white matelasse cotton playsuit, 1936. Straw hat features stripes in red.

Jean Parker wears a honey beige lastex lace trimmed in golden brown waterproofed velvet. The accessories are of natural horsehair cloth trimmed with vari-colored raffia and the hat actually folds into a parasol, 1937.

From *Good Night Ladies* we have **Terry Walker** (top) and **Eleanore Whitney,** 1937.

Patricia Morison, 1937 was a dress designer in New York before entering films in the late 1930s.

Jean Harlow, shortly before her death in 1937 at the age of 26.

June Knight, 1937.

Virginia Dale is best remembered for her performance in *Holiday Inn,* although she appeared in nearly 30 other films.

Joy Hodges,1939.

This wonderful Halloween publicity photograph features **Nan Grey** in pleated shorts with belt loops and a flap pocket.

Dixie Dunbar a specialty dancer as well as an actress, can be remembered as the dancing legs in the Old Gold cigarettes television commercials of the 1950s.

Ruby Keeler and **Al Jolson** were married from 1928 to 1939.

Helen Parrish, 1939.

A young **Lana Turner,** fresh from Hollywood High, on her way to stardom, 1937.

Grace Bradley models backless overalls in heavy brown linen with large white buttons, 1934. Three years later, Grace would become Mrs. William Boyd. That's "Hoppalong Cassidy" to you.

Pauline Moore starred in several Charlie Chan adventures in the 1930s and even appeared uncredited as a bridesmaid in *Frankenstein* in 1931. These clever photos of your typical 1930s creations, were photographed during her stint in modeling.

Margaret Lockwood from England. Photographed during her brief stint in Hollywood, 1939.

Ginger Rogers, 1938. Ginger was very fond of playsuits and flowers making this three-piece shirred suit a sure favorite.

These girls show off some great fashions for the sun. Note the variety of shoes being worn.

Joy Hodges, in a bronze satin lastex with seaweed pattern print in blue, green, and white. Joy is pool side at the El Mirador in Palm Springs, 1938, where she resides today.

Dorothy White sunning at the Beverly Hills Sand and Pool Club, 1938. Although her nearly 10 year career of dancing in films was uncredited, she appeared in such musicals as *Palmy Days* (1931), *42nd Street* (1933), *Gold Diggers* of (1933), and *Down Argentine Way* (1940).

Ben Blue, Laurie Lane, and **Joyce Mathews** (right), in publicity for *Coconut Grove,* 1938. The pleated shorts feature side zippers.

Betty Grable's legs were such an asset to Twentieth Century Fox studios that they insured them with Lloyds of London for one million dollars and thereafter she was known as "the girl with the million dollar legs." She brought a special charm to Fox musicals, most of which were produced in color.

Virginia Bruce made many films between 1929 and 1960 and was once married to screen idol John Gilbert.

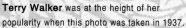

Terry Walker was at the height of her popularity when this photo was taken in 1937.

Gloria Stuart chooses slacks for comfort in this 1936 photograph. Gloria is just as popular today, thanks to "Titanic" , than any other time in her more than 70 years in films.

Helaine Moler, 1938, is another actress who appeared uncredited in films in the late 1930s.

Judith Barrett, 1939, began her career in 1929, as **Nancy Dover.**

This rare photograph of **Claudette Colbert** appeared on postcards in Europe before World War II. Claudette received an Academy Award for *It Happened One Night* in 1934.

Girls from Warner Brothers' *Stage Struck,* 1936.
Ethelreda Leopold is third from the left.

Penny Singleton is best remembered for her portrayal of Blondie in the *Blondie* film series from 1938 to 1950. Younger generations will recognize her voice as that of Jane Jetson from the cartoon series. Lending her charms to radio as well, she still has that remarkably wonderful voice today.

Joan Blondell displays an early example of the lace-up suit. Born in New York, Joan appeared in more than 80 films. You younger kiddies may recognize her from *Grease,* 1978.

Constance Bennett appeared in a bathing suit for the first time on screen in *Topper Takes a Trip*, 1939. Her film career began in, believe it or not, 1916. Her sisters, Barbara and Joan, did quite well in Hollywood as well.

Judy King, Norah Gale, and Harriett Haddon get wet, 1938.

Starlets from *Girls School*, 1938. **Peggy Moran** can be seen reading a magazine in lower right corner while **Martha O'Driscoll** enjoys ice cream at the bottom of the photo.

Nancy Kelly, 1938, first appeared in films in 1926 at the age of five.

Shirley Ross models a one-piece suit of white satin lastex striped in wine and purple from Mabs of Hollywood, 1939.

This starlet's publicity stunt in 1939 actually reflects the sentiments of most actresses at the time.

Rosemary Lane with a wonderful matching jacket. Rosemary toured with Fred Waring's Pennsylvanians with her sister, Priscilla, during the 1930s. Her last film was in 1945.

Ellen Drew and Robert Preston In Santa Barbara, 1939.

(L-R) Diane Arden, Gene Foley,
and Rose Heitner ,1939.

(L-R) Alice Koerner, Marjorie Kane,
and Marie Barde ,1939.

This wardrobe test of **Marjorie Weaver** shows a fine example of a tennis outfit in 1939.

Betty Field, 1939, at the Aguora Ranch location for *Of Mice and Men*.
This is one of the first films for this New Yorker.

Rose Heitner, 1939, model for the statue featured in Earl Carroll's night spot.

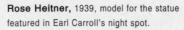

Marsha Hunt and **Leif Erickson,** 1937.

Ellen Drew wears a Ganter Floating Bra suit in velvet lastex knit. This suit cost $5.95 new in 1939. Note the wonderful clogs of cork.

Mary Martin wears a satin lastex with a wonderful western print, 1939. This is one of Mary's first photos taken at Paramount Studios. Mary is best remembered for her roles in *Peter Pan* and *South Pacific* on the stage.

Ginger Rogers ready for tennis in blouse, shorts, and comfortable shoes.

Ina Ray Hutton, 1936.

Muriel Barr, in a suit of gold from 1939, was one of Earl Carroll's beauties before entering her uncredited film career from 1938-1945.

Jean Rogers in athletic attire, 1936.

Margaret Lindsay, 1939.

Carole Lombard, in a pajama suit was tragically killed in a plane crash in 1942 after a bond-selling tour in the mid-west.

Virginia Vale finds a convenient way around the back lot, 1939. Clever Virginia even designed her own costuming for one of her numerous western films.

Dorothy Lamour in satin lastex, 1939.

This satin lastex suit features zipper in back, 1939.

PUBLICITY

During Hollywood's heyday, it was the studios' publicity departments that were responsible for promoting their stars and starlets. The department would come up with anything to get printed. Photographs were staged and captions devised to accompany these photos that were merely dreamed up in someone's head. In one such case, a starlet had gotten married so her studio simply found some old photos of one of the couple's dates and released them as their honeymoon photos. Publicity ranged from clever and amusing to ridiculous but viewed as successful as long as it was printed. Hollywood and the manufacturers of consumer products often worked hand in hand to promote their wares. Child stars, such as Shirley Temple and Sybil Jason even had their own swimsuit products. The following images from photos and magazines represent some of their efforts.

Even a young **Shirley Temple** gets into the act. She actually had her own line of children's swimwear during this time.

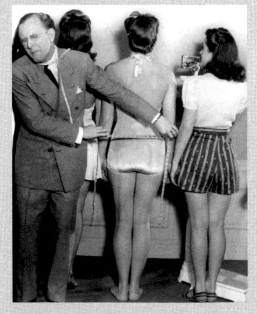

Big band leader, **Kay Kyser,** could always be counted on for a gag, and here he is seen with the "difficult" task of deciding over women, 1940. Kay was a very popular radio personality before entering films with his orchestra in 1939. One of the nice guys of the industry, vocalist Harry Babbit fondly exclaims, "Kay was very generous." Not only did his orchestra have huge hits with novelty and "sweet songs" but they could play some legitimate swing music as well. Kay and these starlets were photographed at RKO Studios.

MGM came up with some "brilliant" publicity for the boys overseas with the use of three baby elephants, **Vicky Lane, Dorothy Morris, Frances Rafferty,** and studio lot 2. These are but two of many photos taken from this ridiculous shoot. In the end, it gained worldwide publicity: Dorothy Morris had her foot stepped upon by an elephant (no serious injury!), and there was photographic proof that women really do play cards, in bathing suits, atop elephants.

(L-R) **Frances Rafferty, Vicky Lane, and Dorthy Morris.**

These "singing secretaries" luckily wore swimsuits under their day clothes enabling them to strip down for comfort in their hot office. Blocks of ice, office fans, and cold drinks help our starlets further their quest in keeping cool in this 1941 publicity including (L-R) **Ella Neal, Barbara Britton,** and **Katharine Booth**. Katharine later became **Karin Booth**.

CASTLE ROCK

hotographers used Castle Rock as a backdrop for many starlets, stars, and would be stars, for most of the first half of the twentieth century. Thomas Ince reportedly first used this site to film William S. Hart. Mack Sennett repeatedly used Castle Rock for his famous bathing beauties, which included Bebe Daniels, Marie Prevost, Gloria Swanson, and Ruth Taylor. Located along the Los Angeles shoreline, Castle Rock was dynamited into the sea in the mid-1940s, deemed a menace for traffic along the "new Roosevelt Speedway" by the California State Highway Department. Castle Rock will forever remain in the thousands of photographs that were taken over the years.

Warner Bros. starlets **Angela Greene, Leza Holland, Suzi Crandall, Joan Winfield,** and **Jane Harker,** 1945.

Esther Williams.

Anne Shirley, 1938. Suit features navy and white striped cotton, closely
fitted bodice fastened with bone buttons, and a full skirt buttoned over tailored shorts.
The tie in her hand is for protection of the mid-section against the sun.

Ann Rutherford wears the same suit at the same location two years later. Original publicity photo caption reads: "Ann has done so much posing on one section of the coast in California that one of the rocks upon which she stands so often has been titled 'Ann Rutherford Rock' by people living in the neighborhood."

Rhonda Fleming displays a Fourth Army Air Force patch during World War II.

Helen Howard walks the beach in a risque suit made from shells, 1941.
It wouldn't be until the 1980s that a suit like this could be bought by catalog.

Sunny Cappy, 1949, models a satin lastex suit will plaid wings—PLAID WINGS!!

To my ~~Low~~ CLASS FRIENDS
HIGH
FROM A LOW DIVER!

Faye

HA-HA-! NO WATER

Faye Emerson was one of Warner Bros. more light-hearted actresses, always clowning around for the cameras or friends. In 1944 her marriage to Elliott Roosevelt, the President's son, brought her great popularity. This photograph was signed by Faye in her usual witty fashion.

The Hays Office

William H. Hays, a former lawyer, was appointed by the major Hollywood studios in 1922 to head the Motion Picture Producers and Distributors of America, Inc. In 1930 the MPPDA created the "Hays Code" to tone down the immorality in films. This code actually listed what could and could not be done in films and was strictly obeyed. It was not a big surprise to see a glimpse of a woman's breast prior to 1930, but with the Hays code sex could not even be implied. Actress Joy Hodges, remembers filming a scene involving a kiss with an actor when "They pulled us aside and said, 'Please keep your mouths closed.' "These standards extended to the various forms of publicity put out by the studios. A photograph or movie poster could not be published or displayed unless it was passed by the MPPDA. The photo below of Joy Hodges was rejected in 1940 because it appeared as though her nipple was showing when in fact, it was a crease in her suit. If printed, however, it may have appeared as the aforementioned. The MPPDA terminated in 1945 and some films seemed to reflect this, but the code remained until 1966. You may wonder what the actor or actress thought about being censored — Joy felt flattered that the MPPDA took time to censor her photo and declared proudly, "Hey, I've been rejected by the Hays Office!"

Magazines

ublicity was realized in thousands of magazines that flourished on newsstands across the U.S. Wonderful fashions could be seen in publications ranging from "girlie magazines," such as *Film Fun* and *Screen Fun* to fashion magazines such as *Mademoiselle.* Servicemen overseas could find their favorite pin-up girls in *Yank* and *Brief.* If you wanted to see your favorite actor or actress in glamour poses, then you purchased one of the many movie magazines. *Motion Picture* offered pin-up gatefolds, while *Movie Life* offered the most photographs of any other magazine. While most movie magazines featured a popular actor or actress on the cover, some, like the 1949 spring issue of *Film Humor* featured three girls on the cover without credit. Two of those girls being Jane Greer and Marilyn Monroe! The following pages are a collective sampling of covers, ads, articles, and pages from the varying magazines of the time frame.

Men of the 390 th Bomb Group, in England, enjoy *Yank* magazine. Esther Williams is the featured pin- up on the back cover.

"RUNNING IMPROVES MY FIGURE?— SILLY, IT'S JUST MY JANTZEN!"

● Presenting the new Jantzen Glamour Fabrics

VELVA-LURE ☆ SUEDE-SHEEN
SATIN-KNITS ☆ KNIT-IN PRINTS

the most radiant stars of summer's bright stage. Their creation is unquestionably the outstanding swim suit news of the year. They are new, amazingly new. They were developed by Jantzen exclusively and are made only *by Jantzen*. Gorgeous textures have been developed in these luxurious Glamour Fabrics. Velva-Lure and Suede-Sheen are soft, gleaming, velvety; Satin-Knits are rich, radiant, lustrous; Knit-in-Prints, of vibrant color and gaiety. *The miracle of Lastex yarn* has been added for just the right amount of two-way stretch that holds the body in youthful sculptured lines. These astonishing tailored Jantzens with Positive Uplift give a new meaning to figure-control in a swim suit for women and set a new standard of trim athletic appearance for men. In the water and out they fit with wrinkle-defying perfection. See these new Jantzen Glamour Swim Suits at your favorite shop or store. Note their rich sheen and beauty of texture. *Feel* their appealing softness. Test their amazing elasticity. Jantzen Knitting Mills, Portland, Oregon; Vancouver, Canada; Sydney, Australia; London, England.

Left: The **ZIP-IN**, a sparkling new Jantzen half-skirt model tailored in gorgeous "Velva-Lure", $7.95. Skirtless model in "Satin-Knit", $5.95. Other Jantzen models, $4.95 to $7.95.

Right: Tops in design, tailoring, fit and fabric in the new **STREAMLINER** in Suede-Sheen, luxuriously soft and rich, $4.95. Other Jantzen trunks $2.95 to $4.95.

Jantzen
MOLDED-FIT SWIM SUITS

JANTZEN KNITTING MILLS, Dept. 229, Portland, Oregon.
Send me style folder in colors, featuring new 1939 models. Women's ☐ Men's ☐

Name
Street   City

1939.

"Tastes best of all!"

says GENE TIERNEY

Star of "A BELL FOR ADANO" a 20th Century-Fox Picture

ROYAL CROWN COLA
BEST BY TASTE-TEST

Gene Tierney

1945.

Styled by MARY ANN DeWEESE *Catalina's Head Designer*   *In Collaboration with Seven World-Famous Hollywood Studio Designers* Creating for Catalina*

**Catalina's 1947 Collection designed by Travis Banton, Universal International Studios; Milo Anderson, Warner Brothers Pictures, Inc.; Edith Head, Paramount Pictures, Inc.; Howard Shoup, who has designed for stars of Metro-Goldwyn-Mayer; Vera West, Universal International Studios; Renie, RKO Radio Pictures, Inc.; Edward Stevenson, RKO Radio Pictures, Inc.—all designing in collaboration with Mary Ann DeWeese, Catalina's Head Designer.*

FULLER Fabric

california in a swim suit

All the golden glory of California—sunny, bright and free—is captured in Catalina's swim suit collection, fashioned for you by the unparalleled stylists of the cinema. Above: talented Mary Ann DeWeese selects a Fuller Fabric of vibrant California prints. Two-piece suit with matching Poncho coat in a wide choice of colors. $15. Write for name of nearest store.

CATALINA SWIM SUITS • SWIM TRUNKS • SWEATERS
Catalina, Inc., Dept. 351, 443 So. San Pedro St., Los Angeles 13, California, U.S.A.

LOOK FOR THE FLYING FISH

Catalina

1947.

1934.

1933.

1947.

1943.

Ann Rutherford, 1942.

Linda Darnell, 1941.

Brenda Joyce, 1940.

Dorothy Jordan, England, 1934.

Joan Crawford, 1939.

Paulette Goddard, 1940.

Dorothy Morris, 1943.

Ginger Rogers, 1944.

1949.

Betty Grable, 1949.

June Haver, 1948.

Diana Lynn, 1947.

1941.

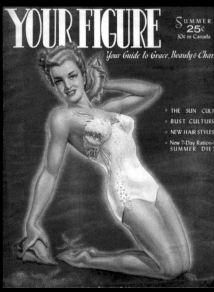

Chili Williams, 1944.

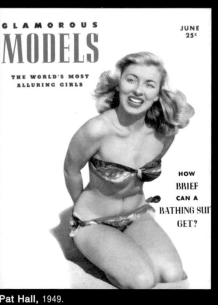

Pat Hall, 1949.

Joyce Reynolds, 1944.

1945.

The Forties

Susan Hayward, 1941.

"I only owned two-piece bathing suits."   - Caren Marsh

"Ernest Bachrach (Photographer)
was one of the sweetest men
I ever worked with."   - Barbara Hale

"The pants suit was a godsend for women."
                                        - Coleen Gray

"Among the many stars and starlets...
some thought it would promote their
careers...some felt that posing in a
bathing suit was embarrassing but
necessary...an obligation to the studio...
so we did it...and some thought it was
just plain fun."   - Joan Leslie

"To me, Cole of California was my favorite
because it was more comfortable and flattering
to my figure."   - Dorothy Morris

Peggy Moran sports this wonderful Catalina one-piece with large bow and jacket of matching material. Peggy was the daughter of famous pin-up artist Earl Moran. This photo appeared in the *L.A. Times,* November, 1940.

Jane Russell, 1942.

Irene Hervey Jones in a game of badminton at her and husband Allan Jones' Bel Air home, 1940.

Linda Hayes, in playsuit of seersucker that features a zipper front, 1940. The shoes are called Huaraches, from Mexico. Linda is the mother of Cathy Lee Crosby

The incomparable **Oliva de Haviland** sports this two-piece in 1940. The multiple Academy Award recipient was not only a gifted dramatic and comedic actress, but had the courage to take on Warner Bros. studios for her right to leave the studio, stemming from her demand for better roles. The lovely lady won.

Jean Carol wears a cotton swimsuit with a long torso effect. It combines a blue and white striped top with a flip skirt of solid blue, 1940.

Ann Rutherford was always Rarin' to go when it came to photo shoots. She could be found on beaches, chairs, walls, rocks, bikes, and even in her own back yard (right).

(Bottom to top) we have **Jeanne Kelly, Anne Nagel,** and **Kay Leslie,** 1940. Jeanne would become Mrs. Richard Brooks.

Gene Tierney, originally from Broadway, will most fondly be remembered for her portrayal of Laura in the film of the same name. She received an Oscar nomination for *Leave Her to Heaven* in 1945. This image from 1940 finds her early in her career.

Marjorie Woodworth.

Earl Carroll was considered to be the authority on beautiful women in the 1930s and 1940s and his nightclub featured women that proved this claim. So successful was Earl that Paramount made a film called *A Night at Earl Carroll's* based on his club. He is seen here choosing some of the girls for that film in 1940. Below, (L-R) are **Claire James, Mildred Sellers, Marion Colby, Anne Roberts, Bobby Woods,** and **Vivian DuBois.**

New Yorker **Jacqueline Dalya,** 1940, appeared in many films including *The Treasure of Sierra Madre,* 1948.

The wonderful **Eleanor Powell** began dancing at the age of eleven. She wed actor Glenn Ford in 1943.

A young **Carole Landis** is photographed at Hal Roach Studios.

Joan Crawford sails the swimming pool!

Anne Baxter ,1942

90

A black one-piece of lastex and **Paulette Goddard** make a wonderful photographic effect.

Wanda McKay's playsuit features a sailboat print, 1940.. Wanda appeared in nearly 50 films from 1939-1952 and appeared in many early television episodes including *The Lone Ranger, Cisco Kid,* and *Range Rider.*

Susan Hayward models a two-piece suit of satin Lastex, 1941.

"For luncheon" add the navy gored street length skirt, with its sash waistband tied at front. Notice the wonderful wood clogs.

Ann Rutherford models a navy and white checked jersey ensemble from 1942. Features swim draped bra and short flared skirt, navy jersey, and navy shorts attached to the skirt.

Betty Jane Rhode's polka dot playsuit is made of cotton. She appeared as a singer in many of her films.

Lynn Bari.

Ida Lupino.

Sonja Henie.

Judy Garland awaits a tennis partner.

Susan Miller, 1941, appeared in *Hellzapoppin,* and *Never Give A Sucker An Even Break,* both in 1941.

Peggy Moran, Helen Parrish, and **Anne Nagel**, looking vibrant and beautiful in their Catalina suits of wool and lastex, 1941.

Paulette Goddard reading *Balzac*.

Beautiful **Janet Blair** poses for one of her first Hollywood photo sessions, 1941. A.L. "Whitey" Schafer is the photographer, and the backdrops are the Beverly Wilshire Hotel and a rooftop in Los Angeles. Previously, Janet was a vocalist with Hal Kemp's Orchestra. She also sang with Tommy Dorsey's Orchestra in 1947's *The Fabulous Dorseys*.

Judy Garland, Hedy Lamarr, and **Lana Turner** from *Ziegfield Girl,* 1941.

1941
RESOLUTIONS
Republic Starlets
RESOLVED:
1. TO STEAL SCENES WHEN POSSIBLE.
2. ALWAYS TO KNOW MY LINES EVEN --
IF I HAVE TO --
UDY THEM.
EVER TO REFUSE SALARY RAISE.
. TO NEVER AGAIN MAKE RESOLUTIO

Madeleine Carroll, 1941, began her film career in the 1920s in England and appeared for the first time in 1936 in the United States. Madeleine returned to England to aid the war effort after her sister was killed in the London Blitz.

Lois Ranson and **Carol Adams** contemplate their New Year's resolutions for 1941.

Canadian born **Alexis Smith** attended Hollywood High before being signed to Warner Bros. in 1940.

For croquet **Joan Leslie** wears this pajama suit in red, white, and blue.

Rita Hayworth made her screen debut in 1935. Dancing since the age of twelve, she would become Columbia studios biggest star. In 1972 Rita appeared in her last film.

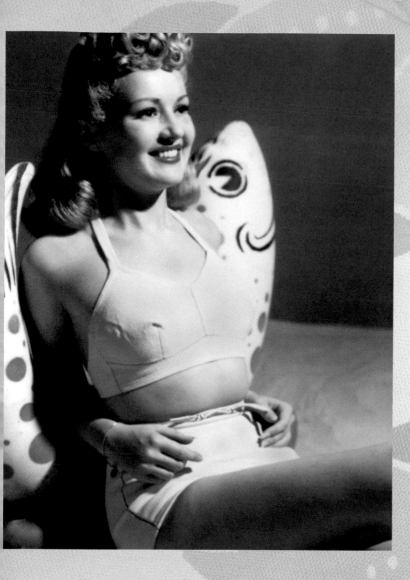

Betty Grable.

Deanna Durbin.

Kathryn Adams strolls Catalina in this white satin lastex sun suit in blue-toned "bursting star" patterns, accented by matching blue silk bra and flared skirt, 1941.

Merle Oberon was born in India.

Paulette Goddard relaxes at home in her flower print playsuit.

Dorothy Lamour was born in New Orleans and, before her movie career, was an elevator operator in Chicago and a radio performer. Her first movie appearance in 1936 was followed by more radio performances, most memorably on the Edger Bergan and Charlie McCarthy show. She is best remembered, however, in Bing Crosby and Bob Hope's "Road" pictures.

Gene Tierney models a midriff blouse in a bold flower print.

Ella Raines, at home, during her second year in Hollywood, 1944. Shorts were very popular in sunwear, especially in California.

Before becoming the 20th century's most famous cowgirl, **Dale Evans** was first seen in *Orchestra Wives*, 1942.

Veronica Lake began her film career as Constance Keane in 1939 and was forever known as the "girl with the peek-a-boo bang" for her unique hairstyle, although others had worn it before.

Ann Miller devoted much of her spare time entertaining the boys in service during WWII. Her unusual bathing suit features lapels and fringed shorts.

George Hurrell snapped this shot of **Ann Savage** at the beginning of her career, 1942. Rubber bathing caps like this were a prized item during wartime rationing.

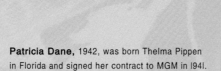

Patricia Dane, 1942, was born Thelma Pippen in Florida and signed her contract to MGM in 1941.

Simone Simon, in a suit of velvet.

Red Skelton having trouble with the ladies in *Ship Ahoy*, 1942.

And now Red charms the ladies in *Thousands Cheer*, 1943.
The starlet in the center is Dorothy Ford.

Marlene Dietrich sports this unusual creation which features a zipper front, belt, padded shoulders, and shorts with matching hand-stitched accents.

Betty Grable listens to the radio in thiscute number. Betty spent many a night listening to the radio while courting Harry James, absolutely entranced by his sweet trumpet sounds over the airwaves. They eventually married in 1943.

Hedy Lamarr.

Ann Sheridan was one of the most popular pin-up girls of World War II.

Dorothy Morris.

Dorothy Lamour.

Nan Wynn, 1943, provided Rita Hayworth's singing voice in many of Rita's musicals. You can find her singing for herself in *Jam Session*, 1944.

Anne Gwynne gives the Army a morale boost at the Hollywood USO, 1943.

Jetsy Parker, Edna May Jones, June Preisser, Eddie Bracken, and **Ruth Gifford** publicize *Sweater Girl* for Paramount, 1942. Poor, unlucky Eddie!

Bob Hope tries to convince **Iris Bynum** that
Bing Crosby is not all that he's cracked up to be.

Gloria DeHaven, 1943, was a popular pin-up girl
for soldiers in World War II. Having a special affection
for anklets, she states, *I'm never without one.*

Born in Hollywood, **Vivian Austin** lent her charms to many
musicals and westerns. Her two-piece features tassels, 1943.

Jean Parker, 1944.

Maria Montez exudes the exotic look in this full-length sarong for *White Savage*, 1943.

Rita Hayworth.

Barbara Stanwyck. This Brooklyn born incomparable, who received an Honorary Academy Award in 1981, was Cecil B De Mille's favorite actress.

Illinois-born **Betty Jane Rhodes,** made her
first film appearance in 1936 as Jane Rhodes.

Frances Rafferty and **Dorothy Morris.** They were the best of friends at MGM studios.

Gloria Jean made her first movie for Universal
in 1939 and is seen here, cute as ever, in 1943.

Dolores Moran in this polka dot two-piece features halter top and shorts with belt.

Jane Wyman was Warner Bros.' busy little blonde of the 1930s and 1940s, appearing in many films. She proved her wonderful talent with her Oscar-winning role in *Johnny Belinda*, 1948. Jane is seen here in a patriotic suit of red, white, and blue, 1940.

Many a soldier fell for **Marjorie Riordan** after seeing her in *Stage Door Canteen*, 1943.

Gene Tierney and a Jantzen two-piece.

Dorothy Lamour cruises Catalina, 1940.

Maria Montez was born in the Dominican Republic and sadly died in 1951. Although the original cause of death was stated as drowning due to heart failure some Hollywood insiders claim it to be a suicide.

Georgia Lee Settle in this Catalina one piece, is as vibrant off screen as she is on. She is seen here in 1943.

Jean Parker models a fine example of a shirred bathing suit, 1944.

Carole Mathews was a model in Chicago and one of Earl Carroll's beauties before breaking into the movies in the early 1940s.

Ann Miller.

Leslie Brooks, publicity for *Cover Girl*, 1944.

Colleen Townsend sports this playsuit for her
Victory Garden, 1944. Colleen's friends fondly
nicknamed her "Coke."

Nancy Marlow sports this one piece with shirred back, 1944.
Nancy has recently written a touching biography of her friend Ruby Keeler.

Wally Brown, Virginia Mayo and Alan Carney in publicity for *Seven Days Ashore*, 1944. The boys' moth-eaten suits date from the 1910s and 1920s.

Marjorie Reynolds.

Mae Craven and Vivien Leigh, 1943.

Carole Landis in St Patrick's Day Victory publicity.

Lucile Ball, 1943.

Betty Hutton, "The Blonde Bombshell" of the 1940s, was a vocalist with the Vincent Lopez orchestra before hitting the big time with Paramount studios in 1941.

Bonita Granville is surrounded by starlets modeling playsuits for *The Song of The Open Road*, 1944. On top is **Peggy O'Neil** and **Bonnie Noland** (right).

Marion Hutton was Glenn Miller's most popular female vocalist and was as vivacious and bursting with energy as her sister, Betty. This photo finds her giving a shot at Hollywood in 1944.

Ann Gillis, 1944, retired from films in 1947 after 13 years in the business.

Marguerite Chapman began her film career in 1940 after having been a "Powers" model in New York. She grew up a tomboy in New York and was known around her neighborhood as "Slugger."

Dolores Moran in publicity for *Hollywood Canteen*, 1944.
This Catalina suit features a tropical fish print in orange and brown.

120

This rare shot of **Maria Montez,** shows her trying on a seersucker, buttoning at the side. Usually these buttons were made of plastic or shell. This candid photo was never released by a studio and therefore never censored.

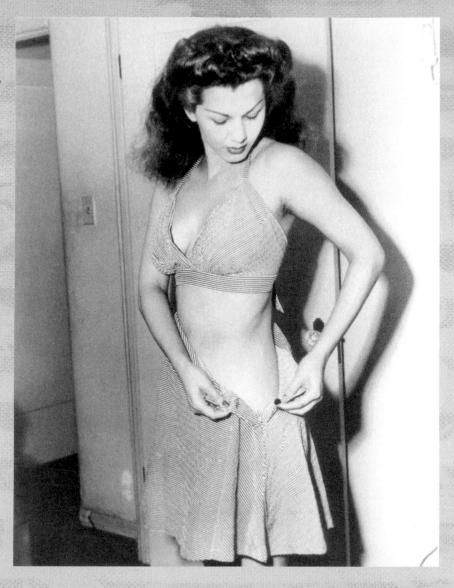

Hedy Lamarr, 1942.

Shelly Mitchell, 1945, was a vocalist for Xavier Cugat and the voice of Axis Sally in *The Story of GI Joe.*

Gloria Jean, 1944. Gloria is 18 years of age here.

Anne Shirley began films at the age of five as Dawn O' Day and was married to actor John Payne between 1937 and 1942. Marsha Hunt and Anne were great friends and could be found running around Hollywood often.

This is **Cyd Charisse's** first publicity for MGM in 1946. She had been a bit actress previously. Ballet fulfilled her life till Hollywood called, where she is remembered today for her many wonderful dance performances through the years. Cyd wed singer Tony Martin in 1948.

Jinx Falkenburg was a swimming and tennis champion before her acting career. The bracelet is made of shells.

Barbara Hale wears this Catalina two piece with halter top. A model before her acting career, Barbara received an Emmy for her work on the "Perry Mason" television series.

Elaine Shepard, 1940.

Barbara Hale and a rayon midriff creation with shorts.
Her film career began during World War II.

Joan Crawford, being helped with the board by a "hidden" person on a beautiful Hawaiian morning.

Marie McDonald was nicknamed "The Body" in the 1940s.

Before being bandleader Kay Kyser's wife and vocalist, lovely **Georgia Carroll** was a bit player in films. Prior to Hollywood, Georgia had a successful modeling career. She appeared in thousands of advertisements, layouts, and on magazine covers in the 1930s and 1940s.

Dorothy Malone, 1949.

Jacqueline White, 1948, in this long sleeved midriff, was sent a valentine of 30 pounds of Delicious Apples from the Washington State Apple Commission. She was chosen as the commission's Hollywood Valentine.

June Haver's suit laces to fit and is gathered at the front. June made her feature film debut in 1943 and married Fred MacMurry ten years later.

126

Priscilla Lane.

Bette Davis.

Baby Jane, 1942.

Dinah Shore, 1941.

This is about the smallest sweater you could get in 1945! It is considered a midriff and has padded shoulders. The shorts feature a zipper and the shoe design is called sling back. The lovely model is **Karen Randall.**

Joan Leslie and **Robert Hutton** in a publicity shot for *Too Young To Know*, 1945.

Marie McDonald tries on a midriff sweater of her own.

Merle Oberon, 1942.

Jane Frazee, a former stage and radio singer, found her niche in Hollywood starring in musicals and westerns in the 1940s.

Joan Leslie gets interviewed by columnist Sidney Skolsky for *Motion Picture Magazine*, 1945. Joan wears a hula skirt over her two-piece bathing suit.

Jo-Carroll Dennison wears a suit by Catalina.
The Army Air Corps insignia is used cleverly as a backdrop.

Betty Grable models the same suit.

Joan Leslie's frock ensemble is made of rayon and her shoes, patent leather.

Janis Paige.

Barbara Hale models a four-piece of cotton.

Jean O'Donnell, Patsy Mace, and **Ethelreda Leopold** from *Bedtime Story*, 1941. Chicago born Ethelreda appeared in more than 50 films in the 1930s and 1940s.

Lynn Merrick in lace-fringed cotton two-piece. Note the wonderful bracelet.

Mildred Coles and Susan Peters, 1941.

Wonderful ensemble with halter top for Trudy Marshall.

Lauren Bacall wears this midriff for relaxing with husband Humphry Bogart. They married in 1945.

Doris Day, 1949.

Eddie Cantor teaching some lovelies a few dance steps.

Starlets from *Easter Parade*, 1948. **Joi Lansing** is at top and **Lola Albright** is top right.

Donna Reed.

Doris Fesette wears a suit made of plastic, 1949.

Bonita Granville looking lovely in satin lastex, 1944. She is 21 years of age.

Olga San Juan, 1945.

Dorothy Morris.

Constance Moore. This stunning actress -singer appeared in no less than 11 films in 1938 alone and is seen even more alluring here in 1945.

Applying suntan oil to **Mary Lou Brue** with a spray gun, 1949.

Laraine Day rarely wore makeup outside the studio.

A joyous **Adele Mara,** in angora sweater, on a fine Los Angeles morning in1943.

Jean Porter, born in Texas, enlivened many films for fifteen years, some of which included her magnificent dancing.

Olga San Juan, 1945, was called "The Puerto Rican Pepper Pot." Of course, she was born in Brooklyn!

Dale Evans adds a western flair with pigtails.

Jeanne Crain gets her lips touched up with a brush. Jeanne was named "Camera Girl of 1942" before her movie career.

Jane Greer made her film debut in 1945 under her real name, Bette jane Greer.

Martha Vickers is remembered as the girl always falling in Bogart's arms in *The Big Sleep*, 1945.

This stylish suit fits **Adele Jergens** like a glove, 1947. Adele first gained publicity as "Miss World's Fairest" at the 1939 World's Fair, having already been a model.

Vera Zorina, 1946. Vera performed many wonderful dances in her films of the late 1930s and 1940s.

Who can forget **Lana Turner's** midriff suit in *The Postman Always Rings Twice*, 1946

142

Yvonne De Carlo is sitting on top of the world, 1945. With the war over, 1946 was indeed something to be happy about, although it was just the beginning of war reparation worldwide. The flags symbolize the allied victory

Jane Greer looks absolutely stunning in this red and white two-piece that lace -adjusts at the waist. She's so stunning, in fact, that you forget she is on a surfboard in the middle of a swimming pool!

Arlene Dahl, modeling a Lee creation, is seen here in 1947, her first year in pictures.

Janis Paige models a Lee bathing suit featuring unusual print from 1947.

144

Caren Marsh's dancing in films goes back to 1937 and she still teaches it today. She was Judy Garland's stand in for *The Wizard of Oz* and has recently written a wonderful autobiography. "The suit was turquoise and white," Caren fondly recalls.

Ava Gardner was signed to MGM studios after someone spotted a photograph of her. Mickey Rooney, Artie Shaw, and Frank Sinatra were her husbands.

Lizabeth Scott was a model before her film career began in 1945.

Shirley Buchanan, 1947, will forever be remembered as the girl on Frank Sinatra's *Songs For Young Lovers* album from 1953. She even turned Frank down for a date.

Pamela Mathews wears a tubbable blue -striped cotton sun frock, 1947.

Marie McDonald in publicity for *Living In A Big Way*, 1947.

Esther Williams, a champion swimmer at 15 years of age, became MGM's "Hollywood Mermaid" and was synonymous with bathing suits. She is seen here publicizing *On an Island With You*, 1948.

Marle Hayden, 1947, appeared uncredited in *Berlin Express* in 1948.

Ella Raines, 1947, wears the hairstyle that would be more synonymous with Bettie Page, who, in fact, would not adopt this until three years later.

Jane Powell, in a two-piece of cotton and clogs of wood. Jane Powell's beautiful soprano voice enriched many MGM musicals.

Beginning in 1934, Marie Wilson played a variety of "dumb blonde" roles and gained great popularity in her radio program "My Friend Irma" which premiered 1947.

These girls appeared in *The Road To Rio*, 1947. (L -R) Marilyn Gray, Dorothy Abbott, Sally Rawlinson, and Kathy Young.

Cheerie Steele, 1949, favors a
haltered two-piece in red polka dots.

These bathing beauties include **Jane Greer,
Faith Domerque, and Jane Russell.**

Adele Mara and a beautiful morning.

Pat Hall modeled and designed her own swimwear like these 1949 creations.

151

Gregg Sherwood models the "Diaper suit," 1949.

Elena Verdugo in publicity from *The Lost Tribe*, 1949.

Linda Christian sports a cotton skirt over her colorful two-piece suit. Beautiful Linda won the heart of Tyrone Power and they were married the year of this photo, 1949.

Peggy Ryan, 1946.

Satin lastex two-piece. Very uniquely designed clogs of wood, 1950.

Barbara Bates, 1949. In a three -piece with halter bra and shorts tailored in black, white, and red cotton print including a long -sleeved shortcoat.

Janet Leigh, 1949.

Jan Sterling, 1950. Jan made her Broadway debut in
1938 but did not make her film debut until 10 years later.

Esther Williams' wardrobe test for *Pagan Love Song,* 1950.

Barbara Osterman was a gifted swimwear designer as well as a model. Her creations leaned towards the brief style (revealing style) and many of her suits were custom fit to the individual's body. She is seen here modeling some of her designs in 1950.

Joyce Reynolds, born in Detroit, smiles at the camera one last time for her final film, *Girl's School*, 1950.

Gwen Caldwell sports a quite revealing suit, 1950.

Cleo Moore, 1950. Movie goers got their first glimpse of vivacious Cleo in 1948.

Gloria Grahame, 1945.

Caren Marsh, 1947. The country girl look is achieved with denim jeans cut into shorts, a popular fad in future years to come. Tied rope serves as a belt.

Coleen Gray, 1950. Coleen's Catalina suit features shirred top and bottom, while the western theme of this photo is promotion for *Apache Drums*. This shot was taken in Apple Valley, California. Fifty years later upon looking at this photo, Coleen laughed hilariously—and who could blame her .

Index